LYRICS of LOVE

God's Top Ten

EDITED BY B. RUSSELL HOLT

Pacific Press Publishing Association
Boise, Idaho
Oshawa, Ontario, Canada

Edited by B. Russell Holt
Designed by Tim Larson
Cover photo by Betty Blue
Type set in 10/12 Century Schoolbook

Library of Congress Catalog Number: 88-63332

ISBN 0-8163-0816-0

88 89 90 91 92 • 5 4 3 2 1

Contents

Preface

Someone has said, "What God gave Moses on Mount Sinai were the Ten Commandments, not the Ten Suggestions."

That's a great line, and it's an even greater truth. God's ten grand principles for living are anything but tentative. The simple words He chose to use have an awe-inspiring certainty about them: "You shall not steal." "You shall not kill." "You shall not commit adultery." "Honor your parents." "Remember the Sabbath and keep it holy." He didn't leave a lot of room for misunderstanding.

Yet neither are the Ten Commandments arbitrary. God wasn't simply trying to demonstrate His authority by telling us what to do. Today, these ancient principles for living—rules some people call them—are as significant for life as they were 3,000 years ago. Timeless. Unchanging. Relevant. Practical.

That's what this book is all about: to show the meaning of God's Ten Commandments for the closing years of the twentieth century, and how they relate to the way you live.

This book began life as a series of eleven articles appearing in *Signs of the Times*—an introductory article, followed by one on each of the commandments. Because they originally appeared as individual magazine articles, the chapters of *Lyrics of Love* have different authors, adding a greater depth to the whole than would be the case if a single author had dealt with all ten.

And as you read, you *will* keep in mind, won't you, that these are commandments, not suggestions?

Chapter 1
Can't We Live As We Please?
Introduction to the Ten Commandments

by B. Russell Holt

When it comes to God's law, a great many people feel that they would be better off without it.

But is that true? Would life really be happier and less complicated if we could get rid of rules and regulations?

Most people think so. The child says to himself, "Just wait until I'm grown like Mom and Dad, and don't have anyone telling me what to do! Then I'll live as I please and enjoy life!"

Mom and Dad are wiser; they know that a person never reaches the point of having no one tell him what to do. But they, too, often think how much happier they would be if they no longer had to pay attention to the restrictions of home, family, society, or even God—if they were free to do whatever they pleased.

It may sound appealing to think of living without rules of any kind, but don't you believe it! That is Satan's line. The truth is that the only person who can be truly happy—truly free—is the person who recognizes that he can't always have

---

Russell Holt is associate editor of *Signs of the Times,* published by Pacific Press in Nampa, Idaho.

his own way. That he has to follow rules and laws.

When I lived near Baltimore, I took my children to Memorial Stadium from time to time to see the Orioles play baseball. I happen to think that a professional ballplayer in action is a thing of grace and beauty. Just watch a double play or a lefthander winding up on the mound or the way the players whip the ball around the bases after an out. It looks so fluid, so effortless.

Once in a while we saw managers arguing with umpires about a call. We saw a few players get angry when they thought a called strike should have been a ball. More frequently we heard fans question the umpire's eyesight or intelligence. But we never saw anyone—fans, players, or managers—arguing that a batter ought to be allowed to stay at bat after three strikes if he wanted to, or that if he preferred, a runner could skip second base and go directly from first to third. A ball game, if anyone is going to enjoy it, has to follow the rules. In fact, there is an *Official Rule Book* that spells it all out in detail. If each player could make up his own set of rules as he went, no one would know what was going on. The game would disintegrate.

And it's not just ball games. Think of the chaos that would take place if everyone were "free" to do whatever he pleased in life. Drivers wouldn't have to stop for red lights if they didn't choose to—but accidents and mangled fenders would certainly increase. The bank teller could decide to cash your check for any amount she chose or not to cash it at all; you would never be sure. The evening news might come at noon one day if Dan Rather decided to take the afternoon off. And the following day there might be none at all.

And what if the laws of nature decided to play fast and loose as well? One morning your toaster works fine because the principles of electricity are behaving themselves, but when you plug it in the next day it incinerates all the wiring in your house. What if you couldn't rely on gravity or sunlight or aerodynamics? Life itself depends on nature behaving orderly.

Obviously, being free doesn't mean allowing everyone to do exactly as he or she pleases. In fact, that's the way to be anything but free. It's the way to tie everyone and everything in knots.

Is it any different with God's laws, the laws that govern our spiritual lives? Not really.

Our well-being depends on obedience to God's spiritual laws just as surely as it does on following the rules that society has agreed upon or as surely as it depends on reliable laws in the natural world. God was not just throwing His weight around at Mount Sinai when He gave the Ten Commandments. He was spelling out how we need to live if we are going to be happy.

Every time I've been sick enough to go to the doctor he has prescribed some kind of medicine. But I don't leave his office muttering, "That doctor sure likes to tell people what to do," as I throw away his prescription. Not if I want to be healthy. The Ten Commandments aren't arbitrary decrees designed to make *God* feel good if we follow them. They are prescriptions intended to make *us* feel good; to keep us free to live happy, productive lives.

Most of us think that the choice we face is this: *Shall I submit to the law or shall I do as I please?* But in a real sense that is not the choice at all. The choice we face is this: *What law shall I choose to follow?* In the natural world, we can't choose whether we want to follow the law of gravity, for example. We can jump off the Golden Gate Bridge, but we will still be obeying gravity.

In spiritual things, the same holds true. "Don't you know," Paul writes, "that when you offer yourselves to someone to obey him as slaves, you are slaves to the one whom you obey—whether you are slaves to sin, which leads to death, or to obedience, which leads to righteousness?" (Romans 6:16).* If we choose to disobey God's spiritual laws, we have simply chosen to obey their flip side—the law of sin that leads to death. Either way we follow one law or the other. Only Jesus can truly make us free. " 'Everyone who sins is a slave to sin. . . . So if the Son sets you free, you will be free indeed' " (John 8:34, 36).

God is not arbitrarily exerting His will when He gives us

His law. He is simply describing how things are, how we can be free and happy.

You see, God doesn't give His law to bad people in order to make them good. He gives it to those He has already redeemed. Notice what He said to the Israelites at Mount Sinai when He announced His law to them: "God spoke all these words: 'I am the Lord your God, who brought you out of Egypt, out of the land of slavery' " (Exodus 20:1). Only after this introduction did He begin to list the Ten Commandments.

This is a significant point. The Ten Commandments were given to a people *who had already been redeemed*, not to people hoping to be redeemed. God had already brought the people out of Egyptian slavery; He had saved them. Now He was telling them how redeemed people ought to live. The purpose of the law is not to provide a way for us to be saved by obedience to it. Its purpose is to describe for us how we ought to live now that God has already saved us by His grace. And there is all the difference in the world between the two.

God first redeemed His people and then gave them His law, thus establishing the principle that the law is primarily for those who are already redeemed. We can see two great spiritual truths in this: (1) We are not saved by our lawkeeping, but by God's grace. (2) It is those who have already been saved who receive the law and obey it. As the apostle Paul put it: "We maintain that a man is justified by faith apart from observing the law. . . . Do we, then, nullify the law by this faith? Not at all! Rather, we uphold the law" (Romans 3:28, 31).

Another writer says it this way: "[God] knows that if He did not make us go to Mount Sinai, we would never go to Calvary. If we do not see our sin, we will not see our Savior. If we will not stand in the searching light of that law, we may not stand in the saving light of that Cross. Mount Calvary is only for those who have been to Mount Sinai" (Peter H. Eldersveld, *Of Law and Love,* Eerdmans, p. 84).

Following this reminder that they were God's redeemed people, the Israelites listened as God outlined in ten great universal principles how redeemed people ought to live. The first four dealt with how they should relate to Him; the last six specified how they should relate to one another. These ten precepts don't cover every specific life situation in detail; you won't find a commandment in the Bible that says, "Thou shalt not attempt to beat the traffic light when it turneth yellow." Instead, the Ten Commandments are drafted in broad terms that apply to every aspect of human experience in all ages and cultures. If we pay attention to their principles, however, we'll know, in most cases, how to relate to contemporary dilemmas—even traffic signals.

If God's law describes how we can live happy and free, why do we find ourselves so often chafing under it?

For one thing, *law* and *sin* are not very palatable words; at least not nearly so much so as *love* and *grace*. Our human nature simply doesn't enjoy hearing about the law. Besides, we have a healthy fear that law will quickly turn into a virulent case of legalism. And, of course, it easily might. Law needs massive doses of grace to inoculate it against such a possibility.

But if we focus on God's love and leave out the ethical and moral content that define that love, we make God One who connives with us *in* our sins rather than One who has acted decisively to save us *from* our sins. The answer is not to emphasize His love and grace less; indeed we need to emphasize them more. But we need to see a God who not only loves, but who, because He loves, cares desperately how His people live. A God who, because He loves, can never agree that sin doesn't matter very much. It is precisely because sin matters so tremendously to God that Jesus dealt with it at such infinite cost to Himself. If sin is of little consequence, if the law doesn't matter, Calvary was a terrible mistake on God's part.

As a pastor, I found that when I began discussing God's law with someone, that person often began bringing up all kinds of arguments and complicated texts to show that the law probably doesn't apply to Christians anymore this side of the cross. Or that if it does, we can't be sure how much of it does or under what circumstances. The whole topic quickly became difficult and obscure.

Mark Twain once said, "Most people are bothered by those

passages of Scripture which they cannot understand. But as for me, I have always noticed that the passages of Scripture which trouble me most are those which I *do* understand."

Irreligious skeptic though he may have been, Twain seems to be saying something important. How many times we puzzle over some obscure text, trying to fathom difficulties that have baffled Bible scholars for centuries. At the same time we willingly bypass the extensive body of Scripture that plainly requires some unwelcome duty or rebukes a pet practice. If we were troubled more by the texts we already understand and less by those we don't, perhaps we would come to understand the latter better.

Of course even the most transparent Bible passage contains unplumbed depths, and we certainly ought to be digging ever deeper into the Word. But isn't it true that the great majority of texts are plain? Isn't it true that we often fail to put into practice even the truth we already know?

The problem usually isn't a lack of knowledge; the problem is more often a lack of willingness to do what we know God's Word says we ought to do. Jesus said, "If anyone chooses to do God's will, he will find out whether my teaching comes from God or whether I speak on my own" (John 7:17).

"Disguise it as they may, the real cause of doubt and skepticism, in most cases, is the love of sin. The teachings and restrictions of God's word are not welcome to the proud, sin-loving heart, and those who are unwilling to obey its requirements are ready to doubt its authority. In order to arrive at truth, we must have a sincere desire to know the truth and a willingness of heart to obey it" (Ellen G. White, *Steps to Christ,* p. 111).

Especially is this true of that section of Scripture in Exodus that we call the Ten Commandments. Willingness makes all the difference. And if we are willing, God has a wonderful plan to make His law even more beneficial to us.

It's one thing to see the law as righteous principles and to agree that we ought to obey them. It's another thing altogether to internalize those principles until they become the expression of how we ourselves feel. That's what God really wants to do with His commandments.

" 'The time is coming,' declares the Lord, 'when I will make a new covenant with the house of Israel and with the house of Judah. It will not be like the covenant I made with their forefathers when I took them by the hand to lead them out of Egypt. . . . This is the covenant I will make with the house of Israel after that time,' declares the Lord. 'I will put my law in their minds and write it on their hearts. I will be their God, and they will be my people' " (Jeremiah 31:31-33).

The law once written on stone is to find a final resting place in our hearts. When it becomes written within—a part of us—it will no longer be an external code which we must try to obey contrary to our natural desires. It becomes a pleasure, the automatic response of the heart to a God of love. "I desire to do your will, O my God; your law is within my heart" (Psalm 40:8, NIV). This is what Jesus was talking about when He said, "If you love me, you will obey what I command" (John 14:15).

"All true obedience comes from the heart. It was heart work with Christ. And if we consent, He will so identify Himself with our thoughts and aims, so blend our hearts and minds into conformity to His will, that when obeying Him we shall be but carrying out our own impulses" (Ellen G. White, *The Desires of Ages,* p. 668).

Now that's really living as you please!

---

*Scripture references in this chapter are from the New International Version.

Chapter 2

Why Does God Have To Be Number One?

The First Commandment

by John C. Brunt

Imagine the following scene: Mike and Elizabeth have dated several times. You can tell by the look in their eyes that they enjoy being together. In fact, they have just returned from a delightful day together. First some playful tennis, then dinner, then a concert. Everything has been perfect. Elizabeth hasn't had such a good time with any of the other fellows she has dated.

Now as Mike walks her from the car to her living room, he pauses, looks into her eyes and says, "I have a command for you. From now on, you shall have no other boyfriends besides me. You will love me and me only. You will date me and me only. Do you understand?"

How do you think this would set with Elizabeth? The tone just doesn't seem right, does it? Something about us doesn't respond very well to commands and demands—especially when it comes to love.

I'm afraid a lot of people feel the same way when they are confronted with God's commands. What kind of God is it who begins the Ten Commandments with the words, "Thou shalt

---

John Brunt is dean, School of Theology, Walla Walla College, College Place, Washington.

have no other gods before me"? (Exodus 20:3, KJV.) Doesn't He know better? Doesn't He know that we don't respond very well to commands and demands? Doesn't this all seem rather arbitrary? How are we to understand and relate to the command, "Thou shalt have no other gods before me"?

I believe we need to keep three things in mind if we are really going to understand this command (as well as the other nine that follow). With these three things in mind, we will recognize that God's demand to be the only God in our lives is not just an arbitrary command.

There really is only one God

The first thing to keep in mind is that there really is only one God. This command is more than just a command; it is a statement of reality.

In our situation above, Mike's command is arbitrary because Elizabeth has a whole world full of eligible young men from which to choose. But the universe is rather limited when it comes to gods—at least to true Gods. There is only one Creator who made us. There is only One who sustains the universe with His power. There is only One who deserves to be called God.

It is an awesome sight to stand at the Acropolis in Athens, Greece. The majesty and beauty of the ruins, well over 2,000 years old, are overwhelming. The ruins, of course, were temples to various Greek gods such as Athena and Nike. The Apostle Paul once stood in Athens in view of all that magnificence when it was not standing in ruins but in its splendor. But Paul spoke not of Athena or Nike. He referred to an inscription he had seen to an unknown God, and he proceeded to tell his listeners about the true God whom they had not known. Notice what he tells us about God:

> The God who made the world and everything in it is the Lord of heaven and earth and does not live in temples built by hands. And he is not served by human hands, as if he needed anything, because he himself gives all men life and breath and everything else. From one man

> he made every nation of men, that they should inhabit the whole earth; and he determined the times set for them and the exact places where they should live. God did this so that men would seek him and perhaps reach out for him and find him, though he is not far from each one of us. "For in him we live and move and have our being." And some of our own poets have said, "We are his offspring" (Acts 17:24-27).*

It is reality, it is a fact—whether we acknowledge it or not, we live and move and have our being in the one true God. There is no substitute. There really is only one God. Therefore, God's command is not arbitrary and exclusive. Rather, it is realistic and true. It is a statement of the reality of the universe.

Worshiping false gods is destructive

We also see that God is not arbitrary when we realize that this command is for our good. The worship of false gods is destructive, for what we worship affects the way we think and ultimately the way we are.

It's easy for us to see this when we think of the ancients. In fact, it's hard for us not to think of them as really stupid. How in the world could they take a piece of wood, carve it, and call it their god? We would expect superstition, lack of understanding, and even moral weakness in people so primitive as to worship pieces of wood and rock.

But obviously idols are not limited to the wooden images of primitive people. Anything that we worship, anything that has our allegiance, anything on which we place ultimate value, is a god. Today, pieces of wood and stone have given way to a polytheism of pleasures. But our false gods are just as destructive, for whenever we give ultimate allegiance to something finite, we weaken our spiritual and moral strength.

Notice what Paul says on this subject. He is speaking of the pagan world of his day, as he shows that both the pagan and the Jewish worlds stand in disobedience to God and in need of His grace:

> For although they knew God, they neither glorified him as God nor gave thanks to him, but their thinking became futile and their foolish hearts were darkened. Although they claimed to be wise, they became fools and exchanged the glory of the immortal God for images made to look like mortal man and birds and animals and reptiles. Therefore God gave them over in the sinful desires of their hearts to sexual impurity for the degrading of their bodies with one another. They exchanged the truth of God for a lie, and worshiped and served created things rather than the Creator—who is forever praised. Amen (Romans 1:21-25).

According to Paul, as people worshiped created things, it made a difference. It led to moral decay. There was nothing to draw them to the moral and spiritual potential that is found only in a relationship with the true God. We become like that which we value. Whenever we worship mere created things, we are drawn to be less than the image of God for which we were created.

God saves before He commands.

There is yet something more that we must keep in mind when we think about the first commandment, "Thou shalt have no other gods before me." We don't really understand this commandment (or any of the other nine for that matter) unless we see the words that immediately precede this command. These words are the forgotten words of the Ten Commandments. They are found in Exodus 20:2. "I am the Lord your God, who brought you out of Egypt, out of the land of slavery."

Leaving out some of the words in the Ten Commandments can be very dangerous. In fact, my parents once found that leaving out just one word can be dangerous. Newly married, they were sitting with several other young couples in a Bible discussion group in their church. All of a sudden one of the women started to laugh. That seemed rather strange, but soon she whispered to my mother who also began to laugh. My father looked over with disgust at these giggling women, but then Mother whispered something to him, and he began to laugh. The laughter went up and down the row until finally the discussion leader wondered what was happening. They finally stopped class, and everyone looked at the culprit. Up in front of the church was a plaque. It had been there for many, many years. It showed two tables of stone, and on it were written the Ten Commandments. But apparently in all the years that plaque had hung at the front of the church, no one had ever read it carefully, for the tenth commandment read, "Thou shalt not covet thy neighbor's house; thou shalt covet thy neighbor's wife." Leaving out just one word made a difference. Needless to say, the next week the plaque was gone.

It is equally dangerous to leave out the words that precede the first commandment. Before God commands that His people shall have no other gods before Him, He reminds them that He is the God who led them out of Egypt and delivered them from their bondage. God commands only after He has acted. He gives the Ten Commandments only after He has acted for His people's salvation.

You see, in the Old Testament, the Exodus from Egypt is the great symbol of God's gracious salvation. In fact, the ceremony that celebrated that occasion, the Passover, would also point forward to Jesus, the ultimate salvation, the Lamb of God who would take away the sin of the world. The Exodus is the great symbol of God's salvation and a symbol of Jesus Christ's ultimate spiritual deliverance from sin.

And so before God says, "Thou shalt have no other gods before me," He says, "I am the Lord your God who brought you out of the land of Egypt." God's grace precedes the law. That puts the whole law in a different perspective. It means that we do not keep the law in order to earn God's salvation. Rather, we keep the law in response to God's salvation. Grace comes first; then we respond with the appropriate thanksgiving and way of life that is worthy of the great salvation that God has provided. That's what Paul means when he makes statements such as these: "Whatever happens, conduct yourselves in a manner worthy of the gospel of Christ"

(Philippians 1:27). "As a prisoner for the Lord, then, I urge you to live a life worthy of the calling you have received" (Ephesians 4:1).

God is our Saviour. In the light of His saving grace, it is foolish to worship anyone or anything else. God saves, and only then does He command. And that gives the command a completely different tone.

We see the same in the life of Jesus. You remember that familiar story. Jesus is confronted by judgmental accusers who bring Him a women caught in the act of adultery. They suggest that the law requires she be stoned. But you remember that Jesus, without saying a word, writes on the ground, and one by one the accusers leave. Finally, when Jesus is left alone with the women, He asks her where her accusers are. And then He says, "Neither do I condemn you. Go and sin no more" (see John 8:11).

Notice how different the tone is than if He had simply said, "Go and sin no more." But it is not only the tone that is different; the theology is different. The theology is right only when the command *follows* God's grace, when our obedience is a response to God's gracious salvation. And that is why Jesus says, "Neither do I condemn you," *before* He says, "Go and sin no more." And that is also why God says, "I am the Lord your God who brought you out of Egypt," before He says, "Thou shalt have no other gods before me."

When we understand this, the first commandment is not an arbitrary, cold, stern command. It is not at all like Mike's command to Elizabeth. It is an expression of the reality of the universe, for there really is only one God. It is an invitation to avoid the destructive worship of false gods, and it is an invitation to respond in the only possibly appropriate way to a loving God who has already acted to save us by His grace.

---

*Unless identified differently, scripture references in this chapter are from the New International Version.

Chapter 3

Four Ways To Spot Your False Gods

The second commandment

by Marvin Moore

Years ago as a kid, my sister climbed a tree in our back yard one day. Finally, she got tired of playing in the tree and began to ease her way back down. She put her weight on a branch, and it broke. Down she crashed to the ground with a thud—and broke her arm. After a quick trip to the hospital, my sister was sporting a brand new cast—a piece of equipment that stayed right with her for the next six weeks or so.

I've thought a lot about my sister's broken arm recently. She put her trust in something that literally "let her down."

Too many Christians are doing much the same thing. Matthew describes them: "Lord, Lord," they'll say to God someday, "did we not prophesy in your name, and in your name drive out demons and perform many miracles?" Then God will say to them, "I never knew you. Away from me, you evildoers!" (Matthew 7:22, 23).*

Take a moment to think about what these people will say: "Lord, we put our trust in our good works. We just knew that they would carry us on through to the kingdom. You surely

---

Marvin Moore is an associate book editor at Pacific Press Publishing Association, Nampa, Idaho.

don't mean that our good works have let us down!"

Unfortunately, that's exactly what God means.

Some people put their trust in something else that will almost certainly let them down someday. Their religion. It doesn't matter whether it's the Buddhist religion, Hinduism, or Islam. They'll all let you down.

"Oh, but I'm a Christian," you say. "Christianity won't let me down."

I've got bad news for you. Christianity won't save you either. Only Christ can do that. If you're putting your confidence for salvation in the fact that you're a Christian, you'll be sadly disappointed someday.

"But I believe in Christ's death on the cross, and the Bible says that we're saved by faith."

Here's more bad news: Faith is not your saviour. Christ is. If you're trusting for salvation in the fact that you believe in Christ's death, let me remind you that the devil believes in His death too. After all, he was there when it happened!

If good works won't save you, and Christianity won't save you, and even faith won't save you, what in the world will?

Only Jesus can save. He is the only One who will ever save you or me or anyone else. Knowing Jesus personally. Making Him our Friend. Trusting Him the way we would our best friend. Even that kind of faith won't save us, but Jesus will save us when we put that kind of faith in Him.

So the important thing is to get to know Jesus personally as a Friend. And the real question is, How do you and I do that?

If you were surprised by what I said earlier, you may be even more surprised by what I say next.

You'll find the basis for a relationship with Jesus right in the Ten Commandments. And I don't mean salvation by works, either. It's in the second commandment.

Did you know that the second commandment is the only one that talks about God's love for us and our love for Him?

"Hold it!" you say. "I thought the second commandment was the one that said, 'Thou shalt not make unto thee any graven image. . . . Thou shalt not bow down thyself to them, nor serve them' " (Exodus 20:4, 5).

You're right, but that's not all that the second commandment says. Read the next few lines two times, very slowly: "I the Lord thy God am a jealous God, visiting the iniquity of the fathers upon the children unto the third and fourth generation of them that hate me, and showing mercy unto thousands of them that love me and keep my commandments" (verses 5, 6).

That is the last part of the second commandment. It tells us that God loves us. He wants to show mercy to us. And that, He says, is the reason why He does *not* want us worshiping idols and images. Because these things can fool us just like the tree branch fooled my sister. They can give us a false sense of spiritual security.

"But I don't worship idols," you say.

Probably not, but I'd like to mention two ways in which Americans and others in the Western world *do* break the second commandment and don't even know it.

I hope you'll understand that what I say next is not intended to be critical of anyone. But where eternal life is concerned it's extremely important to speak out.

Did you know that millions of Christians bow down to images every week, right in church? That's a sad fact, but true. Some churches have images of the saints all around the walls, and usually you'll see an image of the Virgin Mary displayed up front. Now I realize that these Christians say they don't really worship the images in their churches. "These are images of the *saints,*" they say, "not of God. It's just easier to pray to the saints than to God, and we like to be able to see something when we pray."

Let's think about that for a moment. Where does the Bible say to pray to the saints? In His model prayer Jesus told us to pray to "Our Father which art in heaven" (Matthew 6:9). In fact, it's impossible to say, "I don't worship the saints. I just pray to them," because prayer *is* worship. To pray to a saint is to worship that saint, regardless of how much a person may tell himself that it isn't.

Think about this, too: When we pray to someone or something other than God, we begin to depend on that person or thing more than on God.

My conversations with people who pray to the saints in their churches have convinced me that that's exactly what happens. Some have even told me that they are afraid to pray directly to God or Jesus. "God is too holy to approach directly," they say. "We ask the saints to talk to God for us."

But the Bible says, "Let us therefore come boldly unto the throne of grace, that we may obtain mercy, and find grace to help in time of need" (Hebrews 4:16). This verse doesn't say that only the preacher, the rabbi, or the priest is to come to God, but also you and I and all the rest of us common folks. We are to come to Him directly and boldly, without fear. We don't have to go through a saint as a mediator, because the Bible says that Jesus is our Mediator before God.

When you stop to think about it, not only are those who pray before the images of saints in their churches violating God's clear instruction in the second commandment, but they are substituting their own mediator for the Mediator that God provided—the one Who died for them on the cross!

So here's the first way to spot a false god in your life: If you pray in front of images, then according to the Bible you are worshiping a false god.

If you're one of those who prays to images, I'd like to encourage you to take another look at that practice in light of what the Bible says. If you're praying to someone God never told Christians to pray to, and if you're failing to pray to Him personally the way He said you should, doesn't it seem reasonable that you're in danger of putting your trust in the wrong thing? Fortunately, my sister's arm eventually healed after she broke it by putting her trust in the wrong thing. The result of putting your trust in the wrong thing spiritually is much more serious. It may be eternally disastrous.

"But I go to church every week," you say, "and there aren't any images in my church."

I'm glad to know that. But do you remember I said that there are *two* ways we Americans and others in the West violate the second commandment?

Please read on.

"So powerfully does the automobile satisfy our need to

declare ourselves socially and individually that a visitor from a different planet might see the car as a central feature of an almost universal terrestrial religion. The Sunday preening and cleaning of the revered icons is the weekly worship, and the motor show is the annual holy-day celebration of the car."

I didn't say that. *Psychology Today* did, on page 24 of it's June, 1987 issue, in an article titled, "Driving Passion" (by Peter Marsh and Peter Collett).

I wish that cars were the only things we Americans worshiped besides God. Unfortunately, they aren't. We worship sports and sports heroes. We worship our homes. We worship our jobs. Some of us even worship our families.

"You've got to be kidding," you say. "I don't bow down in front of my car or my house or my family and pray to them."

True enough. But bowing down in front of a thing isn't the only way to worship it. Worship is not merely praying to God. Real worship means putting God first in our lives.

Anytime someone or something besides God takes first place in our lives, that someone or something becomes our god.

For example, did you keep checking your watch during the sermon last week, hoping the preacher would quit in time for you to get home and watch the Cowboys beat the Redskins? (Pardon me, I used to live in Texas!)

I don't mean that it's wrong to watch a football game. I'm not even going to criticize you for watching a football game after church, even though I wouldn't do that myself. I wish the issues were so simple that a rule that said, "Don't watch football after church," would take care of everything. The real problem with the person who keeps checking his watch in church, hoping the preacher will quit so he can get out and do something else, is that "something else" is more important in his life than the God he came to church to worship.

So here's another good way to spot the false gods in your life: Anytime you rush through a spiritual exercise so you can get to something else, that something else is more important to you than God. It's your idol.

I wonder if that won't be the problem with those people who say, "Lord, Lord, haven't we done all these wonderful things in Your name? Why won't you save us?" I wonder if maybe they rushed through their devotional time in the morning so they could go visit someone in the hospital or get things ready for next weekend's Girl Scout camping trip or so they could get to work on time.

All good things, to be sure. And more important to them than God. The idol in their lives.

I heard a story once about a Quaker who stood leaning on the fence between his house and the place next door, watching a new neighbor move in. The movers carried in plush living room furniture, expensive wall hangings, and all of the most modern electrical and electronic appliances. There was even a handsome bed for the cat!

At the end of the day, when the last piece of furniture had been moved in and the truck had driven away, the Quaker saw his new neighbor in the yard. He called him over and introduced himself. After they'd talked a while the Quaker said, "By the way, friend, if there's anything you're lacking, let me know and I'll show you how to get along without it."

Materialism. Things. These are the modern idols we worship.

However, please don't think that money and things are wrong in themselves. Jesus did not say that it would be wrong for a man to gain the whole world, but that it would be a sad mistake for him to gain the whole world and lose eternal life (see Mark 8:36). It's not things, but our attitude toward things, that makes them an idol. A wrong attitude toward things can show itself in at least two important ways.

I was a pastor for several years, and I still remember a woman in my first congregation who kept missing church week after week. One day I stopped by the place where she worked and we talked a few minutes. "Pastor," she said, "I know I haven't been to church recently, but honestly, I'm so tired after six days of work that I just can't make it."

This illustrates how closely the Sabbath commandment is related to the one about images. Anything that comes between us and the time we should be spending with God is an idol.

"But my problem is different," you say. "I don't slave away

six days a week so I can stock my house with plush furniture and the latest electronic gadgets. It's all I can do to keep up with the basic bills."

Let me ask you this: What do you think Jesus will say when He comes and you tell Him, "Lord, Lord, you know how hard I had to struggle just to put food on the table and keep a roof over my head. Surely that won't stand in the way of my salvation, will it?" According to Matthew, Jesus will say, "I'm sorry, I never knew you."

Does that sound harsh and uncaring? Remember what Jesus told His disciples one day: "Do not worry, saying 'What shall we eat?' or 'What shall we drink?' or 'What shall we wear?' For the pagans run after all these things, and your heavenly Father knows that you need them. But seek first his kingdom and his righteousness, and all these things will be given to you as well" (Matthew 6:31-33).

God *must* come ahead of the most apparently pressing problem of life.

So the third way to spot the false gods in your life is this: Anything that keeps you so busy you don't have time to study your Bible, pray, and fellowship with other Christians in church (the three basic ways we develop a relationship with Jesus), is your idol—even a crisis like paying next month's bills.

The second commandment strikes at the root of materialism. This problem is so serious that I'd like to give you another good way to tell whether money and things are idols that keep you from having a relationship with Jesus.

How do you feel when the preacher makes a strong offering appeal in church? What kind of emotional reaction do you get when someone knocks on your door or calls you on the phone and asks you to help with some worthy cause?

I've done a bit of door-to-door solicitation for charity, and I get three basic responses: Hostility, indifference, and joy. The hostile person shuts the door in my face without saying a word. Fortunately, most people are not that rude. The indifferent person will at least talk to me. He either says No and shuts the door, or hands me a dollar and shuts the door. But I can always recognize the joyful person by his attitude. He's interested in the cause I represent, even if he can't give a dime. I've seen some joyful people give when I knew they couldn't afford it!

I feel sad anytime someone says to me, "The reason I don't go to church is that all they ever want is my money." The reason I feel sad is because I know this person doesn't understand the joy I get from giving to my church. I honestly don't resent it at all when I hear calls from various directions for help. I wish I could give to them all!

Jesus told us that He presents Himself to us in the form of people in need, and unless we can feel those people's heartache and help to meet their needs cheerfully, we are in great danger of losing our salvation (see Matthew 25:41-46). Of course, you can turn that into a righteousness-by-works trip, and think that *because* you've helped people God must save you. But the point is not just that you did it, but *why* you did it: Because you loved God and His suffering children. It's that love for others that Jesus is looking for, and when he sees it, He says, "I want that person in My kingdom!"

So here's the fourth way to spot the false gods in your life: Suspect money as an idol if you customarily refuse to help with genuine needs because of personal goals that seem more important, particularly if you often feel irritated about appeals for help.

Whether you pray to your idol in church or have a god such as money that you worship without even realizing it, the most important point to keep in mind is that God loves you, and He wants you to love Him. That's why He gave the second commandment—to warn you and me about the things in our lives that can come between us and Him.

If you ask Him, He'll help you spot the false gods in your life and make a total commitment to Him, the only true God, who loves you so much that He sent His only Son to die for you.

---

*Scripture references in this chapter are from the New International Version.

Chapter 4

The Perils of Profanity

The third commandment

by Dan Day

"Expletive deleted." It's a phrase that has found a home in contemporary American vocabulary since Watergate. When the President's secret tapes of White House conversations were made public, one of the most troubling revelations to many was the profanity and crudeness in the language of our nation's leaders. It seemed that nearly every sentence of the taped transcriptions contained an "expletive deleted" ellipsis.

Some people were shocked. How could these men, to whom we had entrusted the nation's future, display such a lack of common decency and respect for the values of our Christian heritage?

Others were surprised that it was an issue at all, since such language is now heard just about everywhere. "What's all the fuss?" they asked. "These leaders didn't mean anything by it; it's just the way people talk these days."

Changing patterns

The everyday language of many Americans is changing. Slang and obscenities have long been with us. Now techno-

---

Dan Day is marketing vice-president of a graphics design firm in Cleveland, Tennessee.

jargon has been added, muddying the waters even further, especially among young people. Today, parents often have no idea what their youngsters are talking about. The latest phrases change so fast even teens have trouble keeping up. And the use of God's name in casual conversation has become so common that an outside observer might well conclude that we are a very religious society.

But the opposite is true.

It used to be, perhaps in fact, or perhaps only in perception, that "gutter language" was restricted to certain classes of people and such places as smoke-filled rooms and rowdy barroom brawls. And it seemed, at least, that only men used profanity and vulgarity—except for so-called loose women who ran in the same circles as these uncultured, vulgar men.

But this, too, is changing, Street language is now common even in what used to be considered relatively cultured circles. The cigarette ads that tell women, "You've come a long way baby," are prophetic. Women are smoking more (and getting more lung cancer), drinking more, using worse language, and generally fitting right into the pattern that used to be associated with the men around them. And the pattern is anything but positive, especially in the casual way God's name is used.

God talk

"God talk." It's a convenient phrase to encompass the frequent references to God the Father, Jesus Christ, and the Holy Spirit—or any other religious terminology utilized in casual conversation without any specific religious intent. It is virtually impossible to live in the secular world today without hearing such references almost constantly.

Of course, many of those who color their everyday language with spiritual terminology do not generally consider that they are swearing, using profanity, or otherwise casting aspersions on anyone's religious perspectives. Often, the very people using God's name in this manner view themselves as quite religious.

The truth is they usually don't even realize they're employing God's name. The words have become, to them, no more than exclamation points in sentences, fillers while they think of the next thing to say.

Yet this too casual use of God's name has an undeniable impact. The third of God's Ten Commandments declares: "Thou shalt not take the name of the Lord thy God in vain; for the Lord will not hold him guiltless that taketh his name in vain" (Exodus 20:7).

Many of us memorized these words as children. They have the ring of familiarity. But what does it really mean to take God's name in vain? The New International Version translates this same passage, "You shall not misuse the name of the Lord your God."

Misusing God's name takes place in many settings. It happens during what we typically call profanity, of course; but it also happens when we wrongfully use God's name to support our claims or certify our statements (such as in taking oaths with the phrase, "so help me God"—and then lying). And it happens when otherwise sincerely religious people become too casual in their use of God's name.

It's clear that God does not take misusing His name quite as casually as some of us do. Otherwise, a prohibition against doing so wouldn't have been included in His ten fundamental laws of human behavior. Have you ever wondered why God is so protective of His name? What does a little casual God talk really hurt?

God's name and God's character

Keep in mind that God's name is synonymous with His character. Today names are primarily a label. But in Old Testament times, parents gave names to identify what a child was like (or what they wanted him to be like). Or a name might describe circumstances surrounding a person's birth. Names were very personal and powerful. To know someone's name was to hold some power over him. Even today, we have echoes of this idea in phrases like getting a "bad name" and "don't do anything to ruin your good name." Character and reputation are tied to our names.

When we misuse God's name, we're misusing Him. Casual

language about God implies a casual attitude toward God Himself. We may protest that we don't *mean* anything by it—yet that's just the point. We're proclaiming that God doesn't mean anything to us. By being careless, we're declaring that we couldn't care less about God. And since caring about God is very central to spiritual life, God takes it very seriously. Not just for His sake, but for ours too.

The impact of words

We typically think of words as vehicles we use to say things. And they are that. But sometimes we're not as sensitive as we should be to what our words say about us. From the way we use words, people infer, correctly or incorrectly, many things about us. They make judgments about our intelligence, our educational level, how cultured we are, what our parents were like, and what our values are. We often don't realize how much of ourselves we're exposing by the words we use and the ways we use them.

Take Jeff, for example. Jeff seemed to have everything. He was president of his father's company, had lots of money, a college degree, and a lovely family. Jeff was also extremely bright and articulate, with a vocabulary as long as your arm. And Jeff was very involved with his church.

Yet, whenever Jeff got around people he thought might be brighter or more capable than he, he was so intimidated that he fell back into patterns of speech that kept him from having to compete directly with them. All of a sudden, this well-educated, urbane man became a down-home country boy.

His grammar fell apart. His vocabulary closed down. He got loud, and offensive. His conversation became filled with crude allusions, often with bigoted or sexually explicit overtones. And he typically began a stream of off-color jokes filled with enough obscenities and profanity to turn the air blue.

Why the change?

Among the many factors involved, a major one was that this was Jeff's way of protecting himself. It was his way of proving he was a "man" and deserving of rubbing shoulders with other "real men." But all he was really doing was showing how insecure and frightened he was.

When our language is filled with profanity, we're telling the world around us far more about ourselves than we realize. We're letting them in on the poverty of our souls. We're unmasked as lost, confused men and women.

Victory over misusing God's name

If you find yourself using God's name too casually, is there anything you can do about it? Of course there is. But it won't necessarily be easy. Speech patterns don't change overnight. Language is one of the most firmly set habit patterns in our lives. But we can change if our motivation is strong enough and we're persistent.

Changing behavior is a complex process. I've written a book about the process, employing psychological and spiritual patterns (*How to Change Your Behavior,* Pacific Press, 1986). The fundamental truth about altering behavior is that we make changes in our lives only when we really want to—when our motivation is strong. That's why it is usually not enough for those around us to want us to change. We have to want it. And the trick is wanting it enough.

So, why should we want to change our use of God's name—want it enough to do something about it? Here are a few suggestions:

Motivation Number One: Whole people need a vital spiritual dimension in their lives, and misusing God's name strikes a damaging blow at closeness with God.

Anyone who has tried to maintain a vigorous spiritual life over a period of time will tell you how delicate the balance is. We need to be spiritual people, but there are so many distracting factors that we don't need the additional encumbrance of verbal confusion about God.

And that's what misusing God's name is.

The nature of spiritual life centers in a vital relationship with God, and all relationships are two-way streets. Misuse of God's name signals a flaw in our side of the relationship. Not only is it bad in and of itself, but it's a red flag to even more serious problems.

The God-man relationship involves love, trust, and commitment. We are not saved by obedience to the Ten Commandments or by avoiding profanity. We are saved by God's grace, through faith in Jesus. But the faith relationship isn't just some paper transaction in which we say, "I believe," and salvation is locked in. The faith relationship is much like a friendship between two people. It may ebb and flow, but it remains in effect as long as the two of them want it.

How long would your friendship with one of your ordinary friends last if you were abusing and misusing him? How real would the friendship be if behind his back you were using his name in a careless, thoughtless manner? A relationship implies two people treating one another with dignity and respect.

Being God's friend involves speaking well of Him.

Motivation Number Two: On the mundane level an enlightened self interest in our own success will show us that we need to develop positive habits about using God's name.

Every person's life is made up of complex interactions with other people—spouses, other family members, business associates, and friends. Our lives also involve many individuals about whom we're not even aware—people who make decisions concerning our future when we don't even know they're being made, people who might bring us opportunities or turn them away from us.

As we noted earlier, all these people evaluate us on the basis of our language. The words we use are their way of peering into our souls and discovering what lies within us. When our language improves, their evaluation of us will improve. People who speak well are considered intelligent, cultured, and responsible. Others tend to treat them with respect. And the opposite is true too.

By making a conscious effort to clean up our language, we will be taking positive steps toward more fully realizing our personal potential. We will show ourselves to be "classy" people, deserving of classy treatment.

Motivation Number Three: Our own maturing self-respect demands that we aspire toward greater sensitivity to the impact our words have on others.

On the surface, it may appear that the issue is common decency and respect for the feelings of others. But at a more fundamental level, it's a matter of our own personal value system. Most people won't tell us when we're offending them by the crudity of our language. They're too polite. But that doesn't mean they aren't distressed.

One of the signs of a truly mature, responsible person is that he cares about the impact on the people around him of what he does and says. And one of the sure signs that someone hasn't reached maturity is when he doesn't care.

It's been my experience in corporate life that the most successful men and women, the real innovators and managers on the American business scene, tend to be extremely refined people. They take the time to pay attention to others and would never consciously do anything crude or offensive. And this isn't just because they're the product of more refined education or born from the privileged classes. It's because they've learned the hard way what my grandmother used to tell me when I was a little child: "You draw more bees with honey than with vinegar."

These men and women have discovered that "what goes around, comes around." You never know when someone you've treated well or poorly will be in a position to return the favor. So it just makes good business sense to treat everyone well.

Deleting the expletive deleted

These motivations for change may not be enough to cause you to want to become more careful about how you use God's name. You may find other, better reasons that come to mind. The key is to remember that life is what we make it. The material we weave into the tapestry of life determines the shape and color of our future. No one can make you change the way you talk. It will happen only when you determine you want your speech to proclaim to the world that you're changing inside.

When Richard Nixon left the White House after the Watergate scandal, it was the first and only time an American President had been driven from office in shame and disrepute. And it happened, to a large degree, because of *words,* missing and evident, on the hours of tapes he had maintained. Words that condemned because of the actions that they described, and words that condemned because of the glimpses they revealed of character flaws in one we respected for the position he held.

The Watergate break-in, as an act of political excess, was bad enough. But the President's efforts to cover up his top aides' involvement was an act of political suicide. In many ways, Nixon's presidency was a good one. His international forays, such as opening China to the larger world, were even exceptional. Yet he will not be remembered for any of that. He will be remembered for Watergate. Words have a way of coming back to haunt us.

"Expletive deleted" is a tragic legacy to leave behind, and it should give us pause as we consider the pattern of our own words. How much better it would be for our lives to stand as a testimony to intelligence, sensitivity, and culture. The words we speak make the testimony for us—even when we don't realize it's happening.

Chapter 5

Jubilee of the World

The fourth commandment

by Charles Scriven

Each week we are reminded, "You are not alone in a hostile place. You are not living your life in vain."

Isaac Bashevis Singer, a Nobel-prize-winning author, has written one of his stories about an old widow, Bessie Popkin. In Singer's story, Bessie lives by herself in the city. Amid the throng, she is anonymous—a single brick in a vast wall. Despite this, or perhaps because of it, she feels threatened and uneasy—like a cat surrounded by dogs. In fact, Bessie is so filled with distrust that she refuses to keep her stocks and bonds in a safe-deposit box at the bank. Why? Because she has convinced herself that the guards there have passkeys and are likely to steal what is hers.

Is our world friendly or unfriendly? Is it a home where you can feel secure and accepted? Or is it a hell?

In the story, Bessie Popkin definitely thinks of life as an unfriendly hell. She feels she is alone—with street urchins, thieves, degenerates, neighbors, "Evil Powers," even bank guards all deployed against her.

Singer's description brings us up short because there is a kind of searing reality about it. If we ourselves are not Bessie

---

Charles Scriven is pastor of the Sligo Seventh-day Adventist Church, Takoma Park, Maryland.

Popkin, we have still seen her troubled face on streets where we have walked. We all know people whose feeling for life has plummeted like a stone into an abyss. We know that sorrow and misery and fear can overwhelm the human heart.

And all of us, even the most fortunate, know personally at least *something* of Bessie Popkin's plight. We worry about loneliness; we dread the power of death. We compare ourselves with others and feel deficient. We peer into the future and fret about our prospects. We confront, not just the fear and discouragement of others, but discouragement and fear in ourselves. And this raises in all of us questions about the true nature of human life. We wonder, especially in moments when we are down, whether life is good or bad. Is life really worth living, considering all the fear and anxiety involved?

There is another way of putting such questions: Who, or what, is at the bottom of things? What is the basic power behind everything? Has some accident thrust us upon earth? Are we here at the whim of some tyrant? As a result of incredible blind chance? Or are we alive because someone loves us? Is our future full of promise?

Human beings have offered both gloomy and cheerful answers to these questions over the course of history. I want to tell you about two such answers; both bear on our heritage as Christians. One is gloomy, and its importance for us lies in the contrast between it and the answer given in the Bible. I'm going to start with the gloomy answer so that the cheerful one will seem just as bright and splendid as it really is.

To begin, then, let's consider ancient Babylon. Like many other people around the world, the ancient Babylonians expressed their basic attitude to life through stories. Among their most important stories was the one of how the world began. It's been preserved on clay tablets so that we can read it for ourselves today.

The people of that ancient time and place took it for granted that there originally existed a divine world populated by petulant, bickering gods. In their "creation story," the Babylonians told how finally a climactic battle took place among these quarreling deities. On one side was Marduk and his allies; on the other his rival, Tiamat, and her supporters.

According to the story, Marduk routed Tiamat. He then (and this is not a pretty story, by the way) split Tiamat's body in two like a fish and created the sky above with half of her body and the earth beneath with the other half. Meanwhile, the gods who had sided with Tiamat prudently declared their loyalty to the new ruler.

Next, according to the story, victorious Marduk announced his intention to build a giant apartment complex for the gods. This place, Marduk said, would be called Babylon—not surprisingly, since this is, you remember, a Babylonian story.

Marduk assigned the main construction work to the gods who had formerly battled against him. At this point some of the details of the story are missing in our records, but it seems that the defeated gods expressed their fear that they were to become mere slaves. That they would be saddled forever with menial, unrewarding labor. They asked Marduk to assure them that this would not happen.

In response, Marduk made a momentous decision. He resolved to create a "lowly, primitive creature" (these are his very words in the document), and he said, "Man shall be his name." That's right. The "lowly, primitive creature" would be called man. That's you and me. Marduk promised that the precise function of this new race would be to save the worried gods from tedious, everlasting labor. Man would be slaves so that the gods, as he put it, "may have rest."

This story expresses an attitude toward life. It is a picture of how the ancient Babylonians felt about themselves. Brought into being by a tyrant, destined from the beginning to be slaves to the gods and to spend their lives in drudgery. For the Babylonians, the ultimate powers, the mysterious forces responsible for their lives in drudgery. For the Babylonians, the ultimate powers, the mysterious forces responsible for their lives, did not care about them, did not seek fellowship with them, did not give them meaningful responsibilities. To them, the universe was essentially hostile and devoid of hope as far as humanity was concerned. What could make the Babylonian's tongue sing or his heart leap high in gladness?

Well, that's one story—the gloomy one. But there is another story, and it offers much in the way of joy. This is the story told by the ancient Hebrews and preserved in the Holy Scriptures.

The Hebrews knew, of course, that evil does bestride our existence—sometimes like a conqueror. Still when they peered into the depths of things, they saw a basis for a joyful affirmation of life. And they expressed this joy in their own creation story. We find it in the book of Genesis. It begins with a striking idea: that one God—and only one—lies behind everything that is. The picture of a world in the clutches of many quarreling deities vanishes. In its place we see a portrait of a single divine will, a stable Sovereign for the universe.

What is even better, this one God has a loving place in His heart for men and women. We are told that He made the heavens and the earth and all living creatures. And then, we are told (in the best surprise of the whole story) that He established a special day as the climax of His creation. "Thus the heavens and the earth were finished, and all the host of them. And on the seventh day God finished his work which he had done, and he rested on the seventh day . . . from all his work which he had done in creation" (Genesis 2:1-3, RSV).

It may seem puzzling at first why such significance should surround the creation of a day—a Sabbath. But remember that the idea of *rest* (that's what the word *Sabbath* means) appears here in Genesis just as it did in the Babylonian creation story. In Genesis, we are told that God "rested" when He finished His work. In a way, this parallels the Babylonian story, except that in the Babylonian story *rest is a luxury reserved for the gods and never for men and women.*

What makes the God of Hebrew faith so different from the petty, stingy gods of the Babylonians? In the Genesis story God *shares* His rest with the men and women He has made. He has fashioned a new race—not to serve as His slaves, but to be His friends. By blessing and making holy a special day in every week, He set apart a time in which He and all that He has created may enjoy restful fellowship together.

The stories of the world's beginning reveal how ancient

peoples viewed their lives, how they looked upon their difficulties in getting along with each other, their worries about food and shelter, their fears about the future. The Babylonian story suggests a community overwhelmed by these problems—filled, like Bessie Popkin, with distrust. The Hebrew story shows a people charged with joy and confidence. Though they worked and sighed and wept like other human beings, they also sang as the book of Psalms demonstrates. Despite sorrow and trouble, their hearts could be happy.

The question "Where do we come from?" put no fear into them. Rather, it instilled courage. That is what their story communicates to us. They understood themselves to be alive on earth not by the whim of some capricious tyrant, but because of the loving will of a loving Creator. The Sabbath was given to them as a regular reassurance that this was so. At the very beginning God had set apart from all the weekdays a special day of friendship between Himself and them. By this they knew their dignity, their place of honor, in the wide and mystifying universe.

Early in the sixth century before Christ, King Nebuchadnezzar of Babylon invaded Judah, taking many captives back to his own country to be forced laborers. (Remember the haunting stories of Daniel and his friends?) Torn from the land God had promised them and thrust into a foreign culture, the Hebrews more than ever needed reassurance that God was still with them. And we know that during this time of crisis, worry, and pain the Sabbath became especially important to them. A great preacher, Ezekiel, rose up among these exiles, urging them to remember the rest day God had made for them. To him, God's message was: "You must keep my sabbaths holy, and they will become a sign between us; so you will know that I am the Lord your God" (Ezekiel 20:20, NEB).

This suggests a way of expressing the meaning of the Sabbath day for us in the twentieth century: It is a *sign* pointing beyond our human struggle and grief to a God who cares about us and who is stronger than every enemy we face. "The Sabbath," wrote Rabbi Heschel in his moving interpretation of the day, "comes like a caress, wiping away fear, sorrow, and somber memories."

You see, then, that the most basic function of the Sabbath is to enhance life by giving meaning to our existence and peace to our souls. Fear of the gods constantly haunted the ancient world. What cruel surprise would be next? And the same fears exist in the modern world wherever faith is absent. The same uncertainty attacks like a sickness. One of the most famous of all poems in the English language expresses the sense of exile and hurt of the nineteenth-century writer Matthew Arnold. It's called "Dover Beach" after the place in England that inspired it. At night, watching the "long line of spray/Where the sea meets the moon-blanch'd land," the poet sees the waves as a symbol of the "ebb and flow of human misery." Finally he exclaims that the world:

> Hath really neither joy, nor love, nor light,
> Nor certitude, nor peace, nor help for pain.

This is a bleak vision indeed, and it can still be found in our century. In a famous story of the 1950s, *On the Road*, the main character tries to find himself in madcap travels across America. Near the end of the story he tells us, "Nobody knows what's going to happen to anybody besides the forlorn rags of growing old."

I don't believe that. When we are with the God who gives us the Sabbath—a special day of fellowship and rest with Him, a special day to remind us that He created us and loves us—things are different. We know where we stand. Every Sabbath is a festival, building up our trust. On the Sabbath we breathe in from God the strength to love one another and the courage to grapple with dismay. On the Sabbath, we sense anew that with the living God there is rest, assurance, joy, and peace.

A passage from Thomas Merton's autobiography movingly shows how life goes flat, especially in the midst of a crisis, without such peace. Merton, who became one of the twentieth-century's most famous converts to Christianity, was at the time a schoolboy of 15, lacking the faith in God that would one day make him whole. His mother had died already, and now cancer of the brain confined his father to a London hospital.

One day Thomas visited his father and noticed that the tumor had raised a huge swelling on his forehead. As he greeted his father, the boy realized from the sick man's confused, unhappy expression that he could no longer even speak. Thomas buried his face in a blanket and wept, and his father wept too.

"What could I make of so much suffering?" he later wrote. "There was no way for me, or for anyone else in the family, to get anything out of it. It was a raw wound for which there was no adequate relief. You had to take it, like an animal."

The grimness of such a picture pierces our souls. We find no peace here, only sadness. It is what a person comes to when, without a sense of God's love, he meets a grinding human crisis such as death. But with the life and peace and fellowship of God, the human soul grows infinitely strong. Jesus' disciples remembered the days and hours before His death as a time when His whole being was luminous with meaning and hope and peace. Their beloved Teacher—who worshiped on the Sabbath day "as his custom was" (Luke 4:16, KJV)—sensed that He was about to die. Yet He approached His end with dignity. His oneness with the Father made Him able to withstand His greatest trial.

Numerous examples of similar courage illuminate even the darkest pages of human history. Many of those so cruelly tested, like Jesus, have shared Sabbath rest with God each week. One such was John Weidner, a little-known Seventh-day Adventist merchant, whose heroism in the dark age of the Nazis saved hundreds of Jews and many Allied airmen. During the war he was beaten, tortured, and threatened with execution because of his activities in organizing escape routes for the hunted. His sister eventually died in a concentration camp. Yet John Weidner didn't shrink from the danger and misery of his work in the resistance movement. Why? "He had that directness, that simplicity of faith," wrote one of his friends, "which made him realize that he was at all times in the hands of a loving God."

Part of the reason, no doubt, was his Sabbath. As the Sabbath helped ancient Israel to realize the steadfast love behind everything that is, so it helped Weidner. He remained whole despite the things that might have swept away his courage. Fear and sorrow could not overwhelm his heart because the fellowship of God was with him.

It is just this sense of God's fellowship that the Sabbath festival reinforces. In bringing rest from labor, it gives rest also from worry, filling the soul with exuberance, with a feeling for life, with trust and joy.

That is what the Sabbath is about. Each week it tells us, "You are not alone in a hostile place. You are not the slave of greedy gods. You are not living your life in vain." Each week the Sabbath tells us, "Your Creator loves you. Your Creator shares His rest with you. Your Creator has made you *somebody* in the broad and starry universe."

That is why for those who hear the music of the Sabbath, the seventh day comes into the life each week like a jubilee. It *is* a jubilee, the jubilee of the world. Every week it is a gift of gladness, a holiday (holy day) to cheer our waiting hearts.

Chapter Six

How Good People Get Over Bad Parents

The fifth commandment

by Dan Day

Cindy's parents always preferred her older sister Lisa. Lisa was a straight "A" student, a class leader to whom everything came easily. She was the apple of her daddy's eye and her mother's pride and joy.

As the middle child, Cindy always felt she got lost in the shuffle. She was never as brilliant as Lisa and never as cute as Baby Faith. She grew up hearing—sometimes in actions, other times in actual words—that she was "dumb and ugly."

Of course, her parents don't remember or acknowledge ever making such comments. They were good, Christian people who loved all their children equally. But Cindy remembers. She will never forget.

It wasn't that Cindy's parents wanted to be cruel. It was just that they allowed their personal preferences, which they didn't even consciously realize they had, to influence what they said and how they treated the children. And that was cruel, regardless of intent.

Even when the girls were grown and had children of their own, Lisa's two daughters were "special" grandchildren, while

---

Dan Day is marketing vice-president of a graphics design firm in Cleveland, Tennessee.

Cindy's son was just an "extra" grandchild. The cycle of insensitive preferential treatment continued as it always had.

However, when Cindy's parents became old and frail, it seemed natural to everyone concerned (except Cindy) that caring for them would fall to her. After all, Lisa was an important lawyer now; she couldn't be expected to give up her career to care for elderly parents. Faith was a free spirit, totally undependable. Who else was left but plodding Cindy? Besides, she was good at this sort of thing—being in the background and taking care of the drudgery. It wouldn't bother her. And there was nothing in her life to prevent her from being the primary care-giver.

It seemed so logical.

But Cindy was angry.

Her parents had never been there for her in the way she needed them. Why should she be expected to be there for them now? It just wasn't fair!

Still, as a Christian, Cindy worried that she ought to feel differently about all this. After all, didn't the fifth commandment read, "Honor your father and your mother?" (Exodus 20:12.) How could she be faithful to God, feeling the way she did about her parents? Her dilemma was a very real one. How does a good person get over having bad parents?

The sad reality

Many of us have very good parents. They've provided us with all the loving and nurture we could ever have asked for. They've provided sage counsel and caring understanding as we've struggled into adulthood. And we owe them tremendously for it.

But not all of us.

Some of us—far too many of us—have had parents like Cindy's. Or worse. What about the children whose parents have molested and abused them? What about the children whose parents have abandoned them? What about the children whose parents have ignored or belittled them—year after year? How are these children supposed to relate to a requirement that they "honor" their parents?

This isn't a trivial question, applicable only to a tiny minority. Recent statistics indicate that nearly 50 percent of women today have been sexually abused before reaching adulthood. Most of them were abused in their own homes—most often by a parent. And it happens with increasing frequency to boys too. This is the "secret" young people are afraid to acknowledge, the tragedy that colors the rest of their lives—and too often turns them into abusers themselves. Millions of young men and women bear permanent psychological scars from the hands of those the Bible tells them to honor.

How can they do it?

How can *you* do it, if you're one with such scars?

The impossible just takes longer

There are no easy answers to overcoming deep-seated feelings of resentment and hurt—especially when the source of these traumas is the person we most need to trust: our mother or our father. There are no easy answers, but there *are* answers.

For some of us, only extensive professional help will make substantial recovery possible. This is a serious consideration for anyone who is having significant difficulty living with the results of parental mistreatment. There are counseling centers in your community where a brief visit with professional and discreet counselors could help you identify the options and possibilities available. Don't be afraid to take advantage of the opportunity professional counseling offers. You *can* get better.

Short of that, however, those of us with less serious difficulties can take several steps that may help. The following suggestions aren't a substitute for therapy. They're spiritual approaches that try to go beyond symptoms to very deep matters in the heart of someone who's been misused. In this sense, they are common-sense spiritual considerations you could easily work out for yourself, were you not so deeply immersed in the trauma of your past.

The following suggestions are all made in light of the biblical command to "honor your father and your mother." Behind this approach is the recognition that it's not enough for us merely to learn how to cope with the way our parents have treated us; that would be only a passive acceptance. We must also learn how to become agents for healing. We must do more than come to tolerate our parents. We must learn to honor them. Because only then will we be wholly free of their negative influence.

How to honor a bad parent

Honoring our parents isn't something to be taken lightly. It's a matter of some depth. It's a matter of principle.

Matters of principle play an important role in the life of a maturing Christian. Yet they can also be misconstrued, causing more problems than they solve.

I had a man in my office recently whose life had collapsed around him. In his mind each of the disastrous miscalculations he'd made in his business and personal life during the past several years had been the result of acting on "principle." He'd taken a stand, repeatedly, on issues involving friends, customers, and lawyers. And his stand was, in his mind, always a matter of principle. Yet, in each case, he'd found himself deeper and deeper in the pit of malaise.

The problem was, he understood well those matters of principle that governed how others were to treat him; he just had trouble with those involving how he should treat others. There were principles involved in what he did. It's just that larger, more important principles were also involved—which he ignored.

Those of us who have been misused as children and young people will never be able to apply the command to honor our parents if we attempt it as a matter of law. The principle of the law is an important one. But it's wholly inadequate for the challenges we face. Commanding us to honor is like commanding us to love. Neither will work if approached as things we *ought* to do, apart from our relationship with God.

The point is, honoring our parents can be approached effectively only from the perspective of far deeper principles of spiritual growth. It's part and parcel with becoming a more mature person in Christ. We can focus on how to relate better to our parents, since this is the point of crisis. But the real way to do it lies within the confines of how we relate better to God. The two are intimately tied together and will be treated so in what follows.

Suggestion Number 1: As a matter of principle, based on your own choice, begin adopting a God's-eye view of your parents.

I've tried to phrase this suggestion very carefully, emphasizing acting on both principle and choice, rather than according to some imposed rule. Admittedly, it's not possible for us to see things exactly the way God does. After all, He's all-powerful and all-knowing. Love is the basis of His character—not ours. He doesn't have any of the pettiness or bitterness that sometimes flows through us. But to the degree that we try, we'll find our perspective remarkably expanded.

Because of what Jesus did at Calvary, God doesn't see any of us as we really are. He doesn't see the ugliness of sin in us, only the beauty of our righteousness in Christ. This fact is the basis on which our entire hope of salvation rests.

The truth is, while God sees us as righteous, underneath the righteous robe of Christ much unrighteousness is still there. It's just covered. And this is true for even the best of us.

When Jesus observed a "righteous" man and a "sinful" one go into the temple to pray one day, he used them as illustrations of the kingdom of God. The righteous man stood up and prayed, "God, I thank you that I am not like all other men." The sinful man wouldn't even raise his eyes to heaven. He just beat his breast and prayed, "God, have mercy on me." Jesus pointed at the so-called sinful man and said, "I tell you that this man, rather than the other, went home justified before God" (Luke 18:10-14, NIV).

Why was this true? Because the "sinful" man realized and admitted his true condition. He asked for acceptance on the terms of mercy, rather than justice. It was a plea God couldn't resist.

It may very well be just for us to see our parents as monsters. They may have earned it. But God sees even them through the eyes of mercy. And so must we. We need to realize just how needy even the most proper of us really is. Yet God loves us. And He loves our parents just as much as He loves us—in spite of all their flaws, which may be many. It's a perspective we need to begin to see and copy.

Suggestion Number 2: Begin extending forgiveness to your parents—not because they deserve it, but on the basis of how much you've been forgiven.

How can you forgive your parents for what they've done? On your own, you may not be able to. Sometimes it just hurts too much.

But think how much God has forgiven you.

Someone undergoing a great personal tragedy once cried out to God, "Where were You, God, when my son died?" And he sensed from God the response, "I was in the same place I was when My Son died." God paid an incomprehensible price for our salvation. He allowed His own Son to be crucified for us. Does He know the pain caused by sinful behavior? You better believe He does.

Yet, He forgives us—even though we made Calvary necessary. He went through the crucifixion knowing the cost in advance and loving those responsible for it! Can you imagine such a thing? I can't. It is completely beyond my comprehension. But I thank God for it. And I'm moved by it. Moved to see people differently from the way I would otherwise see them. When they misuse me, I think about how God has been misused. And it gives me a totally new perspective.

Honoring bad parents is a matter of faith. It goes beyond reason into that realm we can adopt only because we've been touched by God. Whatever our parents may have done to us, it pales in comparison with what God has done for us. And it is out of the deep reservoir of our joy and gratefulness in Christ that we can extend forgiveness to our parents.

Suggestion Number 3: As an act of faith, begin relating to your parents, not on the basis of what they are, but on the basis of what you are, through Christ.

How we relate to people involves specific behaviors we display. But these behaviors stem from attitudes lying beneath the surface. And it is a change in these attitudes which will enable us to display changed behaviors.

Each Christian is in reality a "becomer." We're people who are caught up in God and are in the process of being changed to reflect His likeness. The more time we spend with God through Bible study, devotional experiences, and service to others, the more thoroughly His character is formed in us.

This process of change is a matter of faith. We can't "work it up." It happens naturally, in the context of our growing relationship with God. Yet we'll never exercise this growing capability unless we try—in very specific situations which test us.

Will we fail at times? Of course. But that doesn't lessen the importance of acting on our faith. God is changing us—often in more profound ways than we realize. And when we extend ourselves in acts of Christian generosity, especially toward those who've wronged us, we discover the miracle of God's transforming power. The occasional failures serve to accentuate the profound effects of being with God.

Just as God has treated us better than we deserve, so we can, by faith, treat others better than they deserve—including abusive parents. We're not overlooking or forgetting what they've done. Instead, we're choosing to display what we're becoming in Christ.

Suggestion Number 4: As an outgrowth of your relationship with God, begin looking for opportunities to become agents for reconciliation with your parents.

In approaching how to survive bad parents, we've considered matters of perspective, forgiveness, and relationship. Now we go one step further into the area of true reconciliation.

It is God who reconciles us to Himself (see 2 Corinthians 5:18). We are the guilty party in matters of sin, so we cannot effectively initiate reconciliation, having no ground on which to stand. So God initiates reconciliation. He goes the second mile, doing for us far more than we could ever ask. He reaches across the crevasse of sin and pulls us into His embrace.

But it doesn't end there.

God then enlists us in a ministry of reaching out to others on the basis of our reconciliation. "All this is from God, who reconciled us to himself through Christ and gave us the ministry of reconciliation. . . . And he has committed to us the message of reconciliation" (2 Corinthians 5:18, 19).

God doesn't want us to be satisfied just with becoming more comfortable with the people who have harmed us. He wants to use us as agents to save them from themselves. He wants us to become agents for healing. This may seem an overwhelming concept to you right now. The hurt and pain from betrayal may blind you to the possibilities in Christ. You may say, "I just can't ever see that happening."

But keep in mind that a ministry of reconciliation isn't something God is demanding of us. He's not saying, "You've got to do it, no matter how much it hurts." It's what He offers us—down the road, when His healing has made us far stronger. Becoming ministers of reconciliation is the joy of maturing Christians. It's one of the most remarkable miracles of true spiritual healing—that someone who has been hurt so badly could be so thoroughly healed that he or she could reach out and help to save the one who did the harm.

Those who have wronged us are often so hardened by years of abusing people that even the urge to seek reconciliation is deadened. They're "damaged goods," suffering the ultimate result of their own actions.

Sometimes, there is no one who could possibly penetrate the thick shell of guilt other than one whom they've hurt. The sheer shock of someone they've misused coming back to seek reconciliation may be the only hope for them. And God may choose to use you as His last attempt to salvage a nearly hopeless sinner.

It is a weighty matter, far too demanding for anyone but God. But what a joy it can be to be such a tool in His hands!

The promise of recovery

One who hasn't gone through the trauma of being misused

by a parent can never really understand just how devastating it is. Its implications extend into our adult lives and frequently into the lives of our children.

We need to get past it all.

The way good people get over bad parents is through turning to a great and marvelous God. His love is large enough to swallow up all our hurt. His future for us is big enough to dwarf whatever lies in our past. The brightness of His tomorrow will drive away the shadows of our painful yesterdays.

If you've allowed the things which have been done to you to discolor your life until now, don't let it go on any longer. God promises you a full recovery. Keep in mind that regardless of your human parents, you are fundamentally God's child. He will be to you the parent they never were. He will give you all they withheld. All the love. All the acceptance. And all the hope.

Take Him up on it now, while you still have life to live. Let the rest of your life be lived free of the past—in Christ. Then, at last, you will be a good person who has emerged victorious over having bad parents.

Chapter 7

Raising Cain—the Killer in All of Us

The sixth commandment

by Dwight K. Nelson

The primeval sunlight scatters its gold through the shadowy patchwork of the hushed forest. Silence. It is as if nature itself shudders in muted shock. Gone the wild medleys of the treetop songsters. Stilled are the scampering paws and scattering hooves of the woodland occupants. Dread silence hangs in the air now heavy with the omen of disaster.

And death. The pounding footbeats of a killer at bay shatter the morning quiet. The lone stranger, half running, half staggering, rounds the forest bend, his eyes wild with terror, his hands splattered with scarlet. Gasping for the cool morning air, the youth stumbles at the feet of one of the primordial forest giants, whose dark trunk towers like a condemning tribunal above the heap of a man.

Guilty. His hands taunt his heart. For no forest floor can wipe away his brother's blood that has left its stain in caked crimson on those hands. His hands. The hands of a killer.

As killings go, it had started out innocently. After all, didn't he have a right to be angry with a brother whose behavior seemed to condemn his own blatant, self-centered way of

---

Dwight Nelson is senior pastor, Pioneer Memorial Church, Berrien Springs, Michigan.

living? And besides, he had only meant to teach him a lesson. But now his brother would never learn anything again. He was dead. Left slaughtered in an open field. And Cain had run.

You can run, but you can't flee. "Cain!" The young man wheels around, staring into the misty shadows behind him. There is nothing to see—only Someone to hear. "The Lord said to Cain, 'Where is your brother Abel?' 'I don't know,' he replied. 'Am I my brother's keeper?' The Lord said, 'What have you done? Listen! Your brother's blood cries out to me from the ground' " (Genesis 4:9, 10).*

Can't you hear it, Cain? Your brother's blood cries from the ground that springs crimson with your killing. Listen to it! Moaning from the war-splattered pavement in Belfast or Beirut, sobbing from the drug-rumpled bedsheets of a tenement addict in Los Angeles or London, crying from the alcohol-twisted wreckage of two automobiles beside the road in Toronto or Tokyo, screaming from the fetus-clogged canisters of another abortion clinic in Denver or Delhi. Can't you hear it, Cain? Listen! Your brother's blood cries out to Me from the ground where you spilled it.

And so it is that the tragic tale of a killer named Cain from the east of Eden goes on and on, replayed a billion times on the broken video of human existence. Is it any wonder then that one of the divine words thundered from the summit of a mountain called Sinai has become the most well known of all? Ask someone to recite the Ten Commandments, and he will almost always begin with the sixth—"You shall not murder" (Exodus 20:13). Surely this is the most obvious evil that God has prohibited. Who would dare to challenge it?

And when we hear those words, we all heave a collective sigh of relief, don't we? Because hell will surely freeze over before you or I are ever caught with blood on our hands! We may find the other nine a bit of a struggle, but with confident pride we can announce to God and mankind our utter innocence at being either accomplice or accessory to anything so heinous as murder. Consequently, " 'Thou shalt not murder' bothers most of us about as much as if God had commanded,

'Thou shalt not spit on the moon.' We have never murdered anyone and don't intend to" (Douglas Beyer, *Commandments for Christian Living* [Valley Forge, PA: Judson Press, 1983], p. 43). Spitting on the moon, murdering a man—we have neither appetite nor tendency for either.

But then maybe we need to climb another mountain. For while God gave the letter of the law on Mt. Sinai, He gave the deep and underlying spirit of that law in another sermon on another mount. And so before we smugly hurry on to the seventh commandment, Jesus beckons us from the Sermon on the Mount with a quiet but shattering word: "You have heard that it was said to the people long ago, 'Do not murder, and anyone who murders will be subject to judgment.' But I tell you that anyone who is angry with his brother will be subject to judgment" (Matthew 5:21, 22).

Is anyone still in a hurry? For in this single, sweeping declaration, Jesus lays bare the pulsating heart of the sixth commandment, and what heart is not indicted? According to Jesus, *to kill* and *to murder* are but the ultimate manifestations of the darker emotion, the deeper verb, *to be angry*. Anger is the destroying root; murder is the devastating fruit. Let the root grow unbridled and unchecked, and the fruit is guaranteed.

Take these few cases in point. Dateline: Cleveland, Ohio. Failor Anderson, 56, said she was tired of the football game and stood between the TV set and her boyfriend, Clarence Broadus, also 56. Broadus, incensed at Failor's interruption, warned her several times and then, so the game could go on, grabbed his 12-gauge sawed-off shotgun and blasted his girlfriend to death. Anger was the root; murder the fruit. And this was no game.

Dateline: Greenville, South Carolina. An informal softball match at a community park was broken up by a melee, when one of the team coaches, Willie Lee Spurgeon, 44, disputed the call of the second base umpire, Raymond L. Dawkins, 52. To settle the call the enraged coach shot the umpire to death. Murder was the charge; anger was the cause. And nothing was settled.

Dateline: Hartford, Connecticut. Two long-time friends,

Charles Brown, 32, and John Plaza, 30, described as being like brothers, got into an argument over who discovered America. Brown was so certain he was right that he became wrong, dead wrong, when he grabbed a pitchfork and stabbed his friend to death. Just like brothers? Like Cain and Abel. Murder was the fruit; but anger was the root. No wonder they call it "raising cain." That tragic tale in the beginning continues its baleful litany in human anger and death today.

Jesus was right about anger and murder, wasn't He? Unchecked and unresolved, anger, like a smoldering ember, transforms itself into the smoking gun of murder.

But wait just a minute! We're still off the hook, aren't we? After all we're respectable people of fairly even-keeled self-control. Oh, sure, we raise our voices and our blood pressure now and then. But never our hands. Anger is something we've learned to confine to words, not weapons. So any talk about murder, homicide, manslaughter, suicide, and war's bloody ravaging is plainly foreign to our rather controlled spirits.

Some may talk about the sixth commandment's relevance for abortion, but we're not terribly disturbed with the U.S. rate of three abortions per minute, since that really doesn't affect us, does it? Others discuss the sixth commandment and alcohol consumption, but since we're not one of the nine million alcoholics suffering a living hell in this nation as they kill themselves and others, why get upset? Cigarette smoking, overeating, and the vices of American gluttony—what some call suicide on the installment plan—clearly are sixth commandment implications for others, certainly not us. Right?

So what are law-abiding, respectable citizens like you and me supposed to do with the sixth commandment anyway? God's word about murder on the first mountain or Jesus' word about anger on the second mountain—either way we come off smelling like a rose, don't we?

Or do we? Maybe the rose is plastic. For could it be that the plastic smile of our complacency is unable to mask the numinous uneasiness deep within us over the fact that Jesus has touched a sensitive nerve with His word about a killing anger?

Maybe there are other ways to raise cain today. What about the times we have come dragging through the door after one of those harried and hectic days at the office? Tired, hungry, and ready to snarl at the whole harassing world, we at least had the courtesy to pet Rover as we dragged in. But there she is—blue jeans spotted with dirty dish water, Sissy's used Pamper gingerly held in one hand and Junior's four-wheel Stomper clutched in the other, a wan smile her last brave evidence that she's waited all day for a little supportive affection. Rover got a pat, and what did the wife get? Murder! Oh, nothing that violent to be sure. But with a cutting little stab about supper's-never-ready-on-time, we unleashed all our pent-up frustration with the world outside on the woman inside—and a killing did take place. Her hope for a strong shoulder and a listening ear was killed, carved right out of her heart. Raising cain inside our own four walls. And we all blush.

But then Junior always did make us blush a little, didn't he? All that talk about being a space pilot, a brave scientist exploring the universe. Well, we set him straight, didn't we! In fact, I don't recall him ever talking about it again, do you? Remember that day we talked some sense into the boy by lecturing him on how foolish it was for him to live in a make-believe world of astronauts? Any boy who can't keep his room cleaner than a pigpen doesn't have the brains to rocket through space!

Just a thoughtless dig. But how many dreams have been killed by digs? At home? In the classroom? At the office, garage, or factory? Killed. Done in by an angry hasty word. Painful memories, aren't they, all those times we met Abel out in the field and dumped the corpse of another dream onto the scrap heap of criticism?

Maybe there's more than one way to raise cain.

"Am I my brother's keeper?" was Cain's futile dodge to God's heartbroken query. Cain knew the answer. And so do we. Which may mean that we're not only our sister's and brother's keeper, but that we are also the keepers of their dreams, their hopes, their unique individuality, their privacy, their ambitions, their purity, their peace, their joy, their love, their right to be treated like the noble children of God that they are. Could it be that you and I are God's assigned keepers to all of that in all of them?

Maybe God's word about murder and Jesus' word about anger have a lot to do with His deep respect for the inherent dignity of all human life. When Cain killed Abel, he murdered more than his brother. He killed a son of God. And God's grief-stricken cry, " 'Your brother's blood cries out to me from the ground,' " is sufficient evidence that the heart of Divine Love is intimately bound up with the hearts of the human race. When someone said, "Man is God in effigy," that was more truth than poetry (D. Stuart Briscoe, *Playing by the Rules,* [Old Tappan, N.J.: Fleming H. Revell Company, 1986], p. 99).

Whose heart doesn't get aroused when we watch a foreign mob hoist into the air an old suit of clothes stuffed with straw, tied with a sign "Here is Uncle Sam," and burned before the gaping cameras? Sure, it's only a bunch of cloth and straw. But our emotions are stirred because of whom the effigy represents! "God created man in his own image, . . . male and female he created them" (Genesis 1:27). Think of how the heart of God must break every time one of his children gets burned. "What you have done to them, you have done to Me!" (see Matthew 25:40). Raising cain with the image of God was no light matter in the beginning; it is no little matter now in the end.

Angry with Cain? No, but how God must have been anguished over him. For if Cain, who was just as much a child of God and whom God loved as much as He did Abel, *wasn't* his brother's keeper, then who on earth would be? If not you, if not me, then who?

Our hearts must confess that there is a bit of Cain in all of us. More than we dare admit. Dare we hope for healing? For every violator of the sixth commandment, that's the best news of all! Because in the sad ending to Cain's story we discover the seeds to a new beginning for all of us. Tragically, Cain "went out from the Lord's presence" and founded the earth's first city (Genesis 4:16, 17). And while the antediluvian cities became bastions of human rebellion against God's relentless love, God one day turned that symbol of rebellion into a sign of redemption!

He called them "cities of refuge" (see Numbers 35:6-34). When the children of Israel marched in that Exodus out of Egypt and into the Promised Land, God directed them to establish six strategically located towns in their new homeland. These villages were designated "cities of refuge," for they were to be a protected haven of refuge where those accused of killing another human could flee and be sheltered from vengeance and retribution.

In the protective environs of the city of refuge the killer and his accusers would be granted an impartial hearing by the village judges. If the killing was determined to have been premeditated, then the killer would be turned over for the execution of judgment. But if the killing was determined to be accidental, then the decree declared that the killer be granted protection from his accuser's vengeance *so long as the killer remained in that city of refuge.*

Just some ancient history? Indeed, but it also captures the best news in the world for the killer in all of us! Guilty of hate and anger, we face the charges of the dark Accuser who can even quote the Scriptures to make his devilish point, "Anyone who hates his brother is a murderer!" (1 John 3:15). But what the Accuser tries desperately to make us forget (or to never learn in the first place) is that there is a City of Refuge to whom every killer can flee! Let your heart cling to Jesus' glorious promise, "Whoever comes to me I will never drive away" (John 6:37). Good news! For flung wide are the gates to God's heart of loving refuge: "I am the gate; whoever enters through me will be saved" (John 10:9).

Yes, the accusations are true. Our petty jealousies, our short-fused tempers, our inconsiderate actions, our critical gossiping, our loveless and cold-hearted words have turned us into killers of our own brothers and sisters, our own spouses and children, our own friends and enemies. We have bloodied hands and lips and hearts. Who can deliver us from the curse of Cain? Where can we flee?

"There is now no condemnation for those who are in Christ Jesus" (Romans 8:1). It really is good news, fellow accused: No condemnation for us in that City of Refuge! The heart of the One who looked for Cain longs for you, too, because the offer has never changed. Flee through the gates of His heart, and you will never be condemned.

How can you be sure? Stand at the rocky summit of another mountaintop. There at the foot of a blood-splattered tree, look up. Hanging there with a nailed-open embrace is the One you have heard before. He is the same One who gave the law on one mountain and preached the sermon on another. Now He dies on a third mountain. Why? To demonstrate to your heart the greatest truth of all in crimson colors that can never be forgotten: When God says He loves you, He wants the killer in you to run—straight into His open embrace.

And that's what raises the Cain right out of us.

---

*Scripture references in this chapter are from the New International Version.

Chapter 8

Safe Sex

The seventh commandment

by Ralph E. Neall

Thirty-eight years ago Bea and I stood before the minister in the Chapel of the Roses in Pasadena, California. After talking about love's garden of roses, he asked each of us whether we would love and cherish the other in sickness and in health, in poverty and in wealth, until death should us part. We replied, "I do," and we did!

We have encountered everything he predicted and then some. There was that first little upstairs apartment in Rochester, New York, a year preaching in Bermuda, two lovely children, strange illnesses in Cambodia, war in Vietnam, and now professorships in Lincoln, Nebraska. We never dreamed then where God would lead us.

We promised to love each other and each other only. And we have. Not that we haven't been tempted from time to time. There have been attractive girls in my classroom from year to year and an occasional man with courtly manners who might have caught Bea's eye. But we remembered our vows before God and our friends—how could we break them? Now we're celebrating thirty-eight happy years of marriage.

I wonder how many of today's marriages will last as long?

Ralph Neall is professor of religion at Union College, Lincoln, Nebraska.

You shall not commit adultery

The twentieth century has revolted against this commandment probably more than any of the others. With the advent of antibiotics and the pill, we lost the old reasons for chastity; now the sexual revolution could begin. Society still condemns lying, stealing, and murder, but not adultery. If I steal my neighbor's car, I go to prison. But if I steal his wife, the state pays no attention. Politicians can sleep with actresses and get away with it; trying to cover it up is what seems to ruin their careers.

Adultery has virtually disappeared from our vocabulary. Now it's "having an affair," "recreational sex," or "safe sex." Schools are teaching our children about sex, but the textbooks are "value-free," which means just what it says. They describe various lifestyles, give statistics and results for each, and then let the children choose their own values. Neither the book nor the teacher says that anything is "right" or "wrong." The students conclude that whatever is, is right. Many choose the lowest common denominator.

The Kinsey reports set the stage for this situation. Written as dry reports of scientific research, they became overnight best sellers because they revealed the sexual habits of the multitudes. Suddenly premarital sex was acceptable because so many were doing it. Virginity at the altar became a relic of the past. The Miss America pageant retained its name, but the "Miss" means only that the girls are not married. The Gallup Poll sets the moral standards today.

What are the results?

Donald M. Joy, author of *Bonding: Relationships in the Image of God,* lists twelve steps of bonding that a normal couple take from their first meeting to their ultimate union. These begin with the first glances and long conversations, progress through hand-holding and hugs, and climax with the sexual embrace.

Through the steps of this sequence the couple become bonded to each other in a union that will last. But if they skip some of the steps and rush to the last ones, the bonding is defective. Joy observes that the "furtive touch of love-making episodes . . . having little bonded foundation, tends to leave both persons dissatisfied" (page 46).

When the sexual experience was a holy place reserved for the dedicated, it was a garden of roses, violets, and orchids, a promised land of joy, perfume, color, poetry, and music. Happy were the children who caught glimpses of it in the loving smiles and kisses of their parents.

But now the gates have been thrown open to casual pleasure-seekers who pick the roses and hear the music, but somehow the colors fade and the music goes silent. Intended as a memory of Eden and seal of the family, the garden has become blighted by broken hearts, diseased bodies, and pregnant children.

Casual sex is casual sex, nothing more and sometimes a lot less. Often it's nothing but biology. "Making love" without commitment is not love; sometimes it's not even fun. The "caring relationship" that doesn't care to commit is not really caring. By definition it is not permanent—the back door is always open.

The problem is that while sexual relationships have become easier to have, they have also become infinitely easier to lose. Ingrid Canright, a 1985 graduate of Antioch College in Yellow Springs, Ohio, points out that mobility is the modern, mature approach to sex and the typical pattern is a series of detached, "caring," relationships in which there are few if any expectations. She said that "fear of attachment confounds communication and leads to despair and anger" in those relationships we do attempt. "Our self-defeating solution is to renounce all romantic notions," Canright says. "Slam goes the drawbridge; we are peacefully, if desolately, alone again. It's an isolation that defends against isolation" ("Mom, Dad We're Disengaged," *Antioch Notes,* Spring-Summer, 1985).

It is also dangerous, like the baby blue jay that fell out of its nest in our yard this summer. The mother looked on helplessly as we tried to care for it. It was in great danger on the ground from the neighbor's cat, our sprinkler system, even our lawn mower. We hoped the mother could keep it fed, but after a couple of days we found it dehydrated and dead. It could not live long outside the nest. The same is true of our love bonds. They thrive only in the nest of God's plan for us.

God's Ideal

God knew about families and love and sex a long time ago. After all, He made us! He knew what would give us fulfillment and joy without regrets. He wrote the operating manual for the human race.

When He created the earth, God saw that everything was good with one exception. Moses quoted Him as saying, "It is not good for the man to be alone. I will make a helper suitable for him" (Genesis 2:18).* God left Adam by himself just long enough to feel his lack, and then put him to sleep and took one of his ribs to create a companion for him. When Adam saw Eve for the first time, he exclaimed, "This, this at last, is bone of my bones, and flesh of my own flesh" (Genesis 2:23, Moffatt). Apparently he was delighted with his bride. He cherished and loved her.

When God made us male and female, He invented sex. It was part of the creating that He declared good. "For this reason," we read in Genesis 2:24, "a man will leave his father and mother and be united to his wife, and they will become one flesh." He rejoices when we enjoy His gifts. Our union, of course, involves much more than becoming "one flesh," for we are not only physical, but also mental, social, and spiritual beings. To be truly one, couples must be united in all four aspects of their lives. The sexual union is the frosting on the cake of union in the other areas. Once we have become one, we can never truly become two again without tearing sections of ourselves apart.

God's plan was monogamy: one man and one woman committed for life. They might, of course, be attracted to others; human beings can be drawn to various partners. Wedding vows do not cancel biology. But it is to say that God intended husbands and wives to "forsake all others and cleave only" to each other. God gave us the power of choice.

While complete union between a husband and wife is like Eden restored, it takes time to achieve. No couple becomes truly one on their honeymoon. Oneness is the achievement of a lifetime. In other words, we do not find the garden all planted and blossoming on our wedding day. We make our own gardens. We have to plant, cultivate, and train the tender blooms of love. With loving looks, kind words, and unselfish deeds we nurture tomorrow's harvest. Those who come only to pick, not to plant and cultivate, do not find the brightest blossoms.

The Bible has a lot to say about sex. From Solomon's lovely song (2:3-6) we listen to the bride's description of her lover:

> Like an apple tree among the trees of the forest
> is my lover among the young men.
> I delight to sit in his shade,
> and his fruit is sweet to my taste.
> He has taken me to the banquet hall,
> and his banner over me is love.
> Strengthen me with raisins,
> refresh me with apples,
> for I am faint with love.
> His left arm is under my head,
> and his right arm embraces me.

In the New Testament Paul compares the union between husband and wife to that between Christ and the church. "Husbands ought to love their wives as their own bodies. He who loves his wife loves himself. After all, no one ever hated his own body, but he feeds and cares for it, just as Christ does the church—for we are members of his body. 'For this reason a man will leave his father and mother and be united to his wife, and the two will become one flesh.' This is a profound mystery—but I am talking about Christ and the church" (Ephesians 5:28-32).

On the other hand, the Bible also describes the tragic results of sex outside of God's plan. The sin of David and Bathsheba, though glamorized by Hollywood, had tragic results. Bathsheba's husband was one of David's bravest officers, but David arranged for him to die in battle in a vain attempt to cover up his sin. Then Bathsheba's baby died. And the consequences continued. Burdened with a guilty conscience, David hesitated to correct his growing children when he should have, and they became headstrong and rebellious. Amnon raped his half sister, Tamar, and died at the hands of her brother Absalom. Absalom himself died in a coup against his father a few years later.

Then there was the tragedy of Hosea, the young prophet whose heart was broken when his wife left him and became a slave prostitute. The wonder of the story is that Hosea bought her back when she went on the auction block, took her home, and made her his wife once again. His redeeming love became a symbol of God's love for His wandering people.

The seventh commandment, "You shall not commit adultery" (Exodus 20:14), was intended to prevent such sorrows and protect the security of our homes. God weeps when we weep; His heart is broken with ours. He longs to see us happy in our marriages and our children growing up in stable families. The seventh commandment has both negative and positive aspects. The positive side is, "You shall love your own spouse." The negative is, "You shall not love anyone else's."

Listen again to Solomon as he gives wise advice:

> Let your fountain flow for yourself alone:
> let a young wife be your joy,
> a lovely hind, a charming doe is she;
> let her breasts give you rapture,
> let her love ever ravish you.
> Why be ravished with a loose creature,
> and embrace the bosom of another woman?
> Man's goings are observed by the Eternal,
> he takes account of all his ways
> (Proverbs 5:18-21, Moffatt).

In Old Testament times adultery was counted a crime as well as a sin. Defined as sexual relations with someone who was already married or engaged, the penalty was stoning for both parties (see Deuteronomy 22:22).

The thing that made the difference between proper and improper sex was a formal engagement or marriage ceremony. The pattern of the ceremony might vary from one culture to another, but it was always public. God seems to bless the union which is recognized by the local culture. Sexual relations after a wedding were a blessing. Sexual relations without a wedding were sin.

Some people have claimed there was no wedding when Isaac took Rebekah into his mother's tent, and "she became his wife, and he loved her" (Genesis 24:67). But this claim overlooks the fact that in Isaac's culture the journey into Mesopotamia to find the wife constituted the marriage ceremony.

As time went on, men's understanding of God's plans increased. While polygamy and easy divorce were tolerated in the early centuries, monogamy was held up as the ideal by the prophets, and the last book of the Old Testament says, "Take heed to yourselves, and let none be faithless to the wife of his youth. For I hate divorce, says the Lord the God of Israel, and covering one's garment with violence, says the Lord of hosts. So take heed to yourselves and do not be faithless" (Malachi 2:15, 16, RSV).

In the New Testament Jesus focused on the thought behind the act: "You have heard that it was said, 'Do not commit adultery.' But I tell you that anyone who looks at a woman lustfully has already committed adultery with her in his heart" (Matthew 5:27, 28).

Did Jesus mean that men should try to deny their natural attraction to women? Should they become monks and leave them entirely? This answer, of course, has never solved the problem of lust and was never commanded in the Bible. The answer lies in the word *lustfully,* which is translated elsewhere as *coveting*. Paul uses this same word in Romans 7:7 when he says, "I would not have known what it was to covet if the law had not said, 'Do not covet.' " Jesus is not condemning the normal attraction between the sexes; He condemns satisfying that desire in ways that are contrary to God's plan. The only right way is within the circle of lifelong commitment.

What if one has not known God's plan, and his (or her) garden is already blighted? What if the threads of life are all knotted and tangled?

Fortunately He can take us wherever we are and lift us up toward His ideal. Jesus is the great Healer, Restorer, and Saviour. Scars may remain—broken families cannot always be put back together, and diseases may be incurable. But Jesus is skilled at straightening out tangled lives, giving "beauty instead of ashes, the oil of gladness instead of mourning, and a garment of praise instead of a spirit of despair" (Isaiah 61:30).

How does He do this? God promises that if we confess our sins, He will forgive and cleanse us from all unrighteousness (see 1 John 1:9). Adultery is not the unpardonable sin. Jesus did not condemn the woman taken in adultery (see John 8:1-11), but told her to go and sin no more. He asked a drink of the Samaritan woman who had had five husbands, and even used her to witness of Him to her city. Bathsheba herself, whose husband was killed at David's order, became the mother of Solomon and an ancestor of Jesus.

Yes, Jesus can restore, but He would rather keep us from falling in the first place. He would rather we not learn the woes of evil. He would like us to avoid the scars of sin. He would like us to enjoy His gifts with no regrets.

The only safe sex is sex in accordance with the will of God.

---

*Scripture quotations in this chapter that are not otherwise credited are from the New International Version.

Chapter 9
Beg, Borrow or Steal?
The eighth commandment

by Len McMillan

Salesman A. H. Livingstone wasn't having much success selling high-quality art to hotel managers. His pictures cost more, he admitted, but he felt they were worth it; they turned a plain hotel room into something special.

"Don't you care about the quality of art you give your guests?" he asked a hotel manager in Los Angeles. "Don't you have any standards?"

"I have one standard," the manager replied calmly. "Any picture that goes in one of my rooms has to be too large to fit into a suitcase!"

We can understand the manager's viewpoint when we realize that motels and hotels in America write off approximately $500 million a year to theft. In fact, hotel managers count on one guest in three stealing something during his stay. One New York hotel tallied up 38,000 spoons, 18,000 towels, 355 silver coffee pots, and 1,500 silver finger bowls stolen during just the first 10 months of operation! Each year, 4,600 Bibles are stolen from New York City hotel rooms.

Hotels aren't alone. The average local library loses between 200 and 500 books each year to thieves. Thirty percent of all business failures occur as a direct result of internal theft, ac-

---

Len McMillan, author of several books and articles, is a pastor in Staunton, Virginia.

cording to insurance statistics. Many stores lose 50 percent of their profits from "inventory shrinkage"—a polite term for stealing by employees. Security officials estimate that 9 percent of all employees steal on a regular basis and that more than 75 percent do so irregularly to some degree. In fact, employees steal three times as much as shoplifters. Theft, both inside and outside, costs retailers an estimated 17 percent of their total business income before taxes. Ignoring the eighth commandment seems to have become a way of life in modern society.

Such intentional disregard for the commandment that says, "Thou shalt not steal," has prompted some creative preventive measures. One recent innovation is an enterprising business called T. H. E. F. T. (The Honest Employee Fooling Thieves). The motto of this fledgling business is "Hire Someone to Fire!" For a fee T. H. E. F. T. will provide a "thief"—usually an unemployed actor—who will go to work for an employer and get "caught" stealing. The "thief" is then fired with a great deal of public shouting and screaming. From this unpleasant scene other employees get a not-so-subtle message.

"Our people are prepared to take as much humiliation as the employer sees fit," says founder Rae Wilder. "The idea is that it's much better for the employer to get the message about stealing across by firing an undercover "thief" than to lose an otherwise valuable employee. Suppose you discover that an employee you've had for 20 years is stealing from your supplies or inventory. You can reprimand that person, but he'll just get belligerent. With our system, you can show him you mean business and still not lose his experience."

When God wrote with His own finger, "Thou shalt not steal," the words may have been few, but the implications were vast. "The eighth commandment condemns . . . theft and robbery. It demands strict integrity in the minutest details of the affairs of life. It forbids overreaching in trade, and requires the payment of just debts or wages. It declares that every attempt to advantage oneself by the ignorance, weakness, or misfortune of another is registered as fraud in the books of heaven" (Ellen White, *Patriarchs and Prophets*, p. 309).

If I use my employer's telephone for private calls, am I stealing? If I balance my checkbook on company time, am I stealing? If I deduct more than I am entitled to on my income tax, am I stealing? Many would answer, "It depends on the situation." Yet when we read the commandment there doesn't seem to be any allowance for particular situations that might invalidate its plain, "Thou shalt not steal."

Stealing from others

A father was trying to explain ethics to his son who was soon to go into business. "Suppose a woman comes in and orders $100 worth of material. You wrap it up and give it to her. She pays you with a crisp $100 bill. As she goes out the door, you realize she has mistakenly given you two $100 bills. Now, son, here is where the ethics come in. Should you or shouldn't you tell your partner?"

A good joke, perhaps, but all too typical of how many today reason. Most Christians wouldn't keep the extra $100 bill, but even Christians may think little of stealing in more subtle forms.

A Christian composer was pleased and honored when his home church announced that the choir would sing one of his most famous songs during the church service. His pleasure turned to dismay, however, when he saw the choir singing from photocopies of his music. An estimated 75 to 100 photocopies of music are made for every copy that is sold. That means that for every dollar he earns through royalties, a composer is losing $75 to $100 from theft.

Most of us dismiss making photocopies or taking paper clips or typing paper from the office. These things are incidental to our general focus in life, and so we don't consider them violations of the commandment against stealing. We reason, The little I've taken doesn't amount to enough to matter." But the real question is, Does the smallness of the thing taken lessen the fact that we took something that was not ours?

The item taken may be insignificant, but the greatest loss is the one we sustain ourselves. We are violating the principles of right and wrong and learning to look upon transgression in small matters as though it were no transgression at all. But it is transgression in little things that first leads the soul away from God. Jesus said, He who is faithful in a very little is faithful also in much" (Luke 16:10).*

Stealing from God

Can human beings steal from God? Yes. God asks in Scripture, "Will man rob God? Yet you are robbing me. But you say, 'How are we robbing thee?' In your tithes and offerings" (Malachi 3:8). Our reasons for withholding our tithes and offerings may appear valid on the surface: "I have too many bills this month; God will just have to wait." "I don't like the way the church is spending money." We may convince ourselves, but is God convinced? Excuses don't lessen the stealing; they merely lessen the pain of a distorted conscience.

The story is told of a doctor who was about to retire in the small French village where he had served the people for many years. He had always treated each sick person whether or not he or she could afford the small fee. As retirement day approached, the townspeople wanted to express their gratitude for his long service in their village. The proposal was made that on a given day, each family would bring wine as it was able and pour it into a large barrel in the village square. The wine would then be presented to the doctor as an expression of the town's gratitude.

The evening came, and the barrel of wine was presented to the doctor along with many speeches. Then the people left, and the doctor was alone in the glow of their affection. He went to the barrel and drew off a glass of wine. He sat down beside the fire to enjoy the wine the people had given. He sipped. It tasted like water! He sipped again. It *was* water! He went to the barrel, thinking there must be some mistake. But no, the barrel was filled with water. The truth slowly dawned. Each family in the village had reasoned, "My contribution won't be missed; the little water I substitute will not be noticed. Others will take care of it."

I'm sure it's just a story and never really happened. But it does illustrate the reasoning so many use for withholding tithes and offerings from God.

Not only is each individual to be faithful in giving to God what is His, but those responsible for the financial structure of the church are also to be faithful in handling the tithes and offerings given by each member.

A federal bankruptcy court has ruled that The Bible Speaks, a fundamentalist church, must return $6.6 million received in contributions from Elizabeth Dayton Dovydenas. Mrs. Dovydenas charged that the church used undue influence and fraud to solicit money from her. The pastor, she argued, exploited her by winning her devotion and lying to obtain gifts of stocks and cash. Judge James F. Queenan, Jr. ruled that the pastor was guilty of "clerical deceit, avarice, and subjugation." He concluded, "The church cannot, under the cloak of religion, commit wrongs upon the public."

Improper use of tithes and offerings is also stealing from God. Using the power of the pastor's office to influence others to give to "pet" projects can also be stealing from God. "Jesus entered the temple of God and drove out all who sold and bought in the temple, and he overturned the tables of the money-changers and the seats of those who sold pigeons. He said to them, 'It is written, "My house shall be called a house of prayer;" but you make it a den of robbers' " (Matthew 21:12, 13).

Stealing from ourselves

Zig Ziglar, well-known motivational speaker, tells of a thief, a man named Emanuel Nenger. The year is 1887. The scene is a small neighborhood grocery store. Mr. Nenger is buying some turnip greens. He gives the clerk a $20 bill. As the clerk begins to put the money in the cash drawer to give Mr. Nenger his change, she notices some of the ink from the $20 bill is coming off on her fingers which are damp from the turnip greens. She looks at Mr. Nenger, a man she has known for years. She looks at the smudged bill. This man is a trusted friend; she has known him all her life; he can't be a counterfeiter. She gives Mr. Nenger his change, and he leaves the store.

But $20 is a lot of money in 1887, and eventually the clerk

calls the police. They verify the bill as counterfeit and get a search warrant to look through Mr. Nenger's home. In the attic they find where he is reproducing money. He is a master artist and is *painting* $20 bills with brushes and paint! But also in the attic they find three portraits Nenger had painted. They seized these and eventually sold them at auction for $16,000 (in 1887 currency, remember) or a little more than $5,000 per painting. The irony is that it took Nenger almost as long to paint a $20 bill as it did for him to paint a $5,000 portrait! It's true that Emanuel Nenger was a thief, but the person from whom he stole the most was himself.

Could you and I be doing what Emanuel Nenger did? Are we stealing from ourselves as we steal from others or from God? Are we failing to live up to our God-given potential? Are we resorting to shortcuts to further our careers or our goals? Are we tainting our lives with stolen opportunities, stolen moments, stolen towels, stolen paper clips?

The lives we live daily are building a character for eternity. Jesus said, "Every one then who hears these words of mine and does them will be like a wise man who built his house upon the rock; and the rain fell, and the floods came, and the winds blew and beat upon that house, but it did not fall, because it had been founded on the rock. And every one who hears these words of mine and does not do them will be like a foolish man who built his house upon the sand; and the rain fell, and the floods came, and the winds blew and beat against that house, and it fell; and great was the fall of it" (Matthew 7:24-27).

"Thou shalt not steal," says the commandment. But rephrased in the positive aspect, it really means "You shall live in total honesty with God, with others, and with yourself."

---

*Bible quotations in this chapter are from the Revised Standard Version.

Chapter 10

When the Truth Is a Lie

The ninth commandment

by Alden Thompson

"Thou shalt not hurt thy neighbor—with lies or with the truth. That's the way it is in God's kingdom."

Story #1. Louise was a gentle child, and beautiful—at least she was at the moment, but her father was a violent and unpredictable man. More than once she had paid the price for his outbursts. The telltale marks were on her arms and face. A pretty dress covered the ones on her back.

Three houses down lived the Martins, a retired pastor and his wife. Devout and gentle Christians, the Martins had struck up a friendship with Louise. When the violence in her own home became unbearable, she would slip over to theirs.

Now Louise's dad stood at the Martin's door, fists clenched, eyes blazing. "Is my daughter here?" he shouted.

She was. How should Pastor Martin respond?

Story #2. As John Wilcox drove home, he pondered the bad news from the mechanic. John's sleek little car, just 3,000 miles out of warranty, looked like it was headed for a major

---

Alden Thompson is academic dean at Walla Walla College, College Place, Washington.

engine overhaul. A casual observer wouldn't notice—not yet. But the mechanic was a man of integrity and experience. John knew the cure would cost big bucks.

Another option would be to sell. Hardly a week went by without someone asking John if he would part with his car. It was a popular model, in spotless condition, pampered and polished both inside and out. Furthermore, John could flash a meticulous service record. He had followed the manufacturer's recommendations to a fault.

What should John tell a prospective buyer?

Story #3. Carmen had just returned to the dorm from a shopping trip in town. She had stumbled across a couple of real bargains and could scarcely wait to share her elation with friends on her hall.

"Friends" might not be quite the right word, for Carmen didn't fit in all that well. In polite language, one would say she lacked social graces. She was something of a master at breaking into conversations at the wrong moment and showing up when she was neither invited nor wanted.

As she rushed into the hall with her purchases in hand, she met Debbie, a vivacious and popular girl on campus, but one who was also caring and sensitive. "Look at my new dress," bubbled Carmen. "Don't you like it?" Debbie's heart sank. The fabric was good quality, but the style was dated, and the design would hardly complement Carmen's figure.

Debbie struggled with her feelings about Carmen. She wanted to be helpful; she wanted to be nice. What should she say?

"Thou shalt not bear false witness against thy neighbour" (Exodus 20:16). How does this ninth command help us respond to these three incidents?

Is God telling us in the command simply to love the truth and hate lies? That's part of the story, to be sure. Scripture is uncommonly blunt in that respect. Two of the seven "abominations" which the Lord hates are "a lying tongue" and "a false witness who breathes out lies" (Proverbs 6:16-19,

RSV). The father of lies is the devil (see John 8:44). By contrast, Jesus came "full of grace and truth" (John 1:14), admonishing us to worship God "in spirit and in truth" (John 4:24), and promising that "the truth shall make you free" (John 8:32).

But simply talking about truth and lies captures neither the full thrust of the ninth command nor the spirit of the decalogue as a whole. When we listen to Jesus and the writers of the New Testament, it becomes clear that the *real* focus of the commandments is on the neighbor. Jesus put it this way: "Whatever you wish that men would do to you, do so to them: for this is the law and the prophets" (Matthew 7:12, RSV). Here is Jesus' one-verse summary of the Old Testament, the guiding principle for Pastor Martin, John Wilcox, and Debbie. And for us.

Elsewhere Jesus spoke of two great commands upon which all the others depend: loving God wholeheartedly and loving your neighbor as yourself (see Matthew 22:37-40). Paul claims that the whole law (including the command not to bear false witness) is summed up in that command to love your neighbor as yourself. (see Romans 13:9).

The second table of the decalogue does give us a string of commands dealing with specific wrong acts: killing, adultery, stealing, bearing false witness. But the common thread uniting them all is the focus on the *neighbor,* indeed, on the very *person* of the neighbor. Many biblical scholars believe that even command eight, "Thou shalt not steal," refers in the first instance to the crime of kidnapping (see also Exodus 21:16), a sin against the *person* of the neighbor rather than simply against his *property.* The seriousness of these crimes against the person (murder, adultery, kidnapping, bearing false witness) is underscored by the fact that Old Testament law decreed the death penalty against them.

Jesus summarized the second table of the decalogue positively: "Love your neighbor as yourself." Negatively spoken, it would be simply, "Don't hurt your neighbor."

Suddenly a new and more penetrating light shines on the command, "Thou shalt not bear false witness against thy neighbour." Here is a prohibition, not just against lies, but against even using the truth in such a way as to hurt our neighbor. Whatever we do or say should be *for* our neighbor, not *against.* And from the perspective of Scripture, the most horrifying sin would be to use truth to gain unjust personal advantage at the cost of our neighbor.

In that connection, a revealing commentary on the ninth command is provided in Deuteronomy 19:15-21, a passage spelling out with painful clarity the penalty for bearing false witness: "You shall do to him as he had meant to do to his brother" (Deuteronomy 19:19, RSV).

Here is an important clue that could guide the key actors in our stories. Pastor Martin should imagine himself in the place of Louise, and, indeed, in the place of Louise's angry father. John Wilcox should put himself in the shoes of a prospective car buyer. Debbie should imagine herself in Carmen's place.

Now let them hear the command: "Thou shalt not hurt thy neighbor." And now let them act accordingly, doing or saying nothing that would hurt another to their own advantage.

For John Wilcox, the answer is straightforward: the truth will be momentarily costly to him personally, but his responsibility to God and to his neighbor is clear. His is not an "intellectual" difficulty, but the "practical" problem of struggling with human selfishness. And that is precisely the point of the command and also where we stumble most often. It is a sobering commentary on our human existence that clear-cut circumstances are often the ones which most easily tempt us to sin.

Turning to Debbic and Carmen, we find a story that illustrates the potential of using the "truth" against a neighbor. Debbie could easily destroy Carmen with a blunt rendition of the facts. But not to tell the truth could leave a struggling human being to make the same mistakes again and again. For Debbie to know how much to tell—and when—demands a double portion of God's grace.

If we tell the truth with evil intent and acid tongue, and thereby destroy a person, we most certainly have broken the ninth command, even though we are "telling the truth." Invoking the penalty clause from Deuteronomy 19:19 clarifies our thinking marvelously: Are we ready for others to treat us as we have treated them?

Of our three stories, the one involving Pastor Martin is the most difficult. I know of no easy answers for him. Yet faithful Christians constantly face such situations in this sin-twisted world. Where do they go for an answer?

Typically, Christians have appealed to the story of Rahab, the town prostitute in Jericho, who had to decide what to say in order to provide cover for the Israelite spies. See Joshua 2. But Rahab was a Canaanite and a prostitute. Is she a reliable witness and example?

Fortunately, there are other examples in Scripture which reveal how God's people have sought to fulfill the spirit of the ninth command in the face of difficult circumstances. These examples can provide guidance for us. But in all circumstances, we must allow the key summary statements from Scripture to reverberate through our minds: Love your neighbor as yourself; treat him as you would want to be treated. In short, don't hurt your neighbor.

Now let's take a closer look at some Old Testament incidents that illustrate how God's people understood the limits and proper application of the ninth command.

Samuel and King Saul (1 Samuel 16:1-3). When God told Samuel to go anoint one of Jesse's sons as successor to Saul, Samuel spoke frankly to the Lord: "Saul will kill me if he hears about it." The Lord responded: "Take a heifer with you, and say, I have come to sacrifice to the Lord" (1 Samuel 16:2, RSV).

Samuel did as the Lord instructed, telling the truth, though not all of it. Because Saul was under demonic influence, the Lord directed Samuel to be very careful with his words. The result: innocent lives were preserved and Saul was spared the additional crime of shedding innocent blood.

The Shunammite Woman and Elisha (2 Kings 4:11-37). Here is a tender story with delicate insight. The Shunammite woman had received the gift of a miracle son, only to lose him again as a result of a sunstroke. She saddled her ass and headed fullspeed for Elisha. He saw her coming and sent his servant Gehazi to greet her and to ask if all was well on the home front.

Gehazi met her and asked his questions as Elisha had requested. "Everything's fine," she responded. Only when she came to the man she trusted, Elisha, did she unburden her heart. It would have done more damage than good to bare her soul to Gehazi. He didn't need to know her agony of heart. Elisha was the one who could help.

Is it possible that when our lives are in turmoil and someone asks how things are, a cheerful-sounding "Everything's fine" may be the best way to love our neighbor—until we arrive at the feet of Elisha, someone who knows and understands?

Elisha and the King of Syria (2 Kings 6:11-23). In a story both frightful and delightful, we find a biblical precedent for "surprise" parties. The king of Syria set out to capture Elisha because the prophet kept giving away the secrets of war. When the Syrian army surrounded the town (much to the dismay of Elisha's servant), Elisha asked the Lord to strike the army with blindness. Then the prophet happily declared: "This isn't the place. Come. I'll take you to the man you want" (2 Kings 6:19).

Surprise. The army opened its eyes in Samaria, in the presence of the Israelite king. "Shall I smite them?" he asked. "Of course not," returned Elisha. Throw a feast for them and send them home."

As a result of Elisha's playful trick, "the Syrians came no more on raids into the land of Israel" (2 Kings 6:23, RSV). Two nations were saved from further bloodshed.

But, you say, couldn't these stories result in a dangerous carelessness with the truth? Indeed. That is a frightening possibility. While it may be right to withhold the truth for the purpose of saving innocent lives (or even to throw a surprise party!), a great danger lurks therein. Telling the truth is habit-forming. So is telling lies. In God's new kingdom there will be only truth and full disclosure—always. I want neighbors of integrity, ones I can trust. Don't you?

And that is precisely the problem in this sinful world, for, with our twisted minds, we may whittle away the principle of truth until nothing remains. Light and darkness blend into a hazy twilight, and we no longer are capable of telling right from wrong. That is why it is so important to make a habit of telling the truth.

Langdon Gilkey, in his insightful commentary on a World War II Asian internment camp, *Shantung Compound,* describes a tragic case where a father proudly touted his son's ability to work the black market with the Chinese farmers outside the camp. Black marketing was forbidden by the captors, but was deemed acceptable by the captives. To the father's horror, however, he discovered one day that his boy had lost the ability to tell the difference between captors and captives. He no longer told the truth to anyone. Something insidious begins to happen when we shade the truth, even for good cause, and no one knows where it will end.

So in our dilemmas we must constantly seek God's guidance. And Jesus' summary statements of the law can help us keep first things first. Indeed, stating the ninth command as "Thou shalt not hurt thy neighbor" is in keeping with the context of the decalogue and the Old Testament, and in harmony with the spirit of the law as expressed by Jesus.

And in that very connection, let's return to Pastor Martin, John Wilcox, and Debbie, and ask what counsel we might have for them in light of a command which reads: "Thou shalt not hurt thy neighbor."

Pastor Martin, we have no clear counsel for you. Whatever you say could be catastrophic. May your relationship with God and your understanding of His Word be your guide in that terrible moment when you must say something. And may God grant you grace to love your neighbor as yourself—both innocent Louise and her violent father.

John Wilcox, put yourself in your neighbor's shoes. Sell the car if you must, but don't do anything that would hurt your neighbor.

Debbie, you know the frustrations you have had with Carmen over the months. On the one hand, you could be mightily tempted right now to "tell the truth" in such a way as to destroy her. On the other hand, you could avoid the problem and pass her by with a superficial greeting. But that would not give her the help she needs. Quick, pleasant words now could hurt her in the end. So love her as you would want to be loved. Jesus would like that.

Thou shalt not hurt thy neighbor—with lies or with the truth. That's the way it is in God's kingdom. Deep inside, we all know that is the way it should be.

---

*Unless otherwise noted, scripture references in this chapter are from the New International Version.

Chapter 11

Thought Crime

The tenth commandment

by Clifford Goldstein

In his fictional nightmare *1984,* George Orwell created a society that punished illegal thoughts. Winston Smith, Orwell's main character, knew that even if he never breathed a word of what he was thinking, he had already committed the unforgivable crime: wrong thoughts.

"The Thought Police would get him just the same. He had committed—would still have committed, even if he never set pen to paper—the essential crime that contained all others in itself. Thoughtcrime, they called it. Thoughtcrime was not a thing that could be concealed forever. You might dodge successfully for a while, even for years, but sooner or later they were bound to get you."

Fortunately, Orwell's predictions about *1984* proved ultra-pessimistic. Such totalitarian control of thought processes themselves has never come to pass.

God, on the other hand, *can* read our minds, and He is interested in our thoughts. But unlike the leaders of Orwell's fascist fantasy land, who destroyed those who harbored "wrong" thought, God doesn't want to punish us for the evil that trespasses through our minds. Instead, He wants to change our thoughts, to bring them into harmony with His own thoughts of compassion, mercy, and self-sacrificing love.

Clifford Goldstein is editor of *Shabbat Shalom,* Washington, D.C.

He wants to make these changes because He knows that if our hearts are pure, the rest of us will be too. "Keep thy heart with all diligence," says Proverbs 4:23, "for out of it are the issues of life."

For this reason, the tenth commandment towers over the rest. The first nine deal with actions, words, and physical manifestations of the thoughts that stir within. People don't steal, commit adultery, or kill unless first the thought originates in the mind, where it sprouts, grows, and finally ripens into the act itself. The same is true of using the Lord's name in vain, bearing false witness, or dishonoring parents. The first nine commandments deal with outward actions and words, but the tenth makes the transition from this physical world into the realm of the imagination, into the mysterious dimension of the soul. The tenth commandment deals with our thoughts alone apart from our actions.

Of course, thoughts and deeds are linked. The thought is to the act as the egg is to the chick. You can't have the act without first the thought, any more than you can have a chick without first the egg. The tenth commandment is God's attempt to crush the egg before the chick ever hatches. "You shall not covet your neighbor's house. You shall not covet your neighbor's wife, or his manservant or maidservant, his ox or donkey, or anything that belongs to your neighbor" (Exodus 20:17, NIV).

But God is not like Orwell's Thought Police. He wants us to think, to use our minds. He prohibits only certain thoughts. And His prohibition is not arbitrary; it deals only with covetousness. And not even every type of covetousness, because not all covetousness is evil. The psalmist exclaims, "My soul longeth, yea, even fainteth for the courts of the Lord: my heart and my flesh crieth out for the living God" (Psalm 84:2). Like him, we may safely covet a relationship with God. The tenth commandment forbids coveting only that which does not, and should not, belong to us. We have no right to our neighbor's wife; therefore we have no right even to desire her. Both the deed and the desire are sin.

"All the passions of the soul which spur and shake it out of its proper nature and do not let it continue in sound health are hard to deal with," wrote the Jewish philosopher Philo, who lived at the time of Jesus, "but desire is the hardest of all."

Greed, covetousness, desire are not just ancient passions. If anything, greed has become almost an art form today, a philosophy, a way of life. "Greed is all right," announced former Wall Street arbitrageur Ivan Boesky during his commencement address at the University of California School of Business Administration in 1985. "Greed is healthy. You can be greedy and still feel good about yourself." Boesky should know. The year before his arrest for inside stock trading, he made $100 million on Wall Street.

What we think—not just what we say or do—has consequences because what we think often translates into action. Just ask Ivan Boesky. The tenth commandment, therefore, serves as a hedge against trampling upon the rest. A person who obeys the tenth commandment will be better prepared to obey the first nine; a person who breaks the tenth is ripe to break any of them.

The tenth commandment is actually the legal formula for the basic biblical truth that God is concerned with our innermost being. "The Lord seeth not as man seeth," says the Bible, "for man looketh on the outward appearance, but the Lord looketh on the heart" (1 Samuel 16:7). David wrote, "O Lord, thou hast searched me, and known me. Thou knowest my downsitting and mine uprising, thou understandest my thoughts afar off" (Psalm 139:1, 2).

God's Ten Commandment law towers over man-made legal codes because it deals with our thoughts, our motives, our innermost intents. No law in America can do that; God alone can discern the secrets of the soul. "For thou, even thou only, knowest the hearts of all the children of men" (1 Kings 8:39). Human laws legislate actions and sometimes words—lying in court, for example, is illegal. But God is calling us to a law that transcends the action—a legal code for the mind itself.

This principle bears on the very essence of Christianity. When asked what is the greatest commandment, Jesus replied, "Thou shalt love the Lord thy God with all thy heart, and with all thy soul, and with all thy mind. This is the first and great commandment. And the second is like unto it, Thou shalt love thy neighbour as thyself. On these two commandments hang all the law and the prophets" (Matthew 22:37-40).

Both deal with love—an emotion, a thought, a stirring of the heart. Like the tenth commandment, these two principles—love to God and love to man—are concerned with what goes on inside where God alone can see. Jesus hangs all the law and prophets on not just our actions, but on our thoughts themselves. No wonder God is concerned with the heart!

For many of us, the idea that we can be condemned for our thoughts is terrifying. If apart from committing the act man is guilty simply by lusting in the heart, who is innocent? If God knows the evil that lurks within and judges us guilty of that evil even if it never comes out, who can stand in the day of judgment? Paul warns, "This ye know, that no whoremonger, nor unclean person, nor covetous man, who is an idolater, hath any inheritance in the kingdom of Christ and of God" (Ephesians 5:5).

If, then, wrong thoughts alone are sin, all humanity stands condemned before God. We all, like Winston Smith, are guilty of Thoughtcrime. "Do not imagine that you will save yourself, Winston, however completely you surrender to us," said O'Brien, Winston's captor. "No one who has once gone astray is ever spared. . . . We shall crush you down to the point where there is no coming back."

Though we, too, have gone astray, God deals differently with us. All of us who have committed Thoughtcrime (or any other crime) can be spared, can be saved, thanks to Jesus Christ who has died in our behalf. "God commended his love toward us, in that, while we were yet sinners, Christ died for us" (Romans 5:8).

Because Jesus became a human being with us, lived with us and shared our temptations, He can sympathize with our struggles. "In that he himself hath suffered being tempted, he is able to succour them that are tempted" (Hebrews 2:18). God "knoweth our frame; he remembereth that we are dust" (Psalm 103:14).

Jesus not only faced the same temptations we face, He overcame those temptations. "We do not have a high priest who is unable to sympathize with our weaknesses, but we have one who has been tempted in every way, just as we are—yet was without sin" (Hebrews 4:15, NIV). And through Jesus, we can overcome temptation as well. The good news of the gospel is that besides forgiving our sins, Jesus gives us power to overcome them—all of them, even Thoughtcrime.

God will cleanse us from the filth and debris that have accumulated in the cracks and crevices of our brains. He wants to sweep away the trash that poisons our lives. He wants to purge the stains on our souls. He wants not to just heal our broken hearts but to create new hearts within us. And upon these new hearts—not upon tablets of stone—He wants to write His law. "I will put my law in their inward parts, and write it in their hearts; and I will be their God, and they shall be my people" (Jeremiah 31:33).

Many have longed for this change in their lives. "Create in me a clean heart, O God; and renew a right spirit within me" (Psalm 51:10). Search me, O God, and know my heart: try me, and know my thoughts: and see if there be any wicked way in me, and lead me in the way everlasting" (Psalm 139:23, 24).

And these longed-for changes can take place. Let the wicked forsake his way, and the unrighteous man his thoughts: and let him return unto the Lord, and he will have mercy upon him; and to our God, for he will abundantly pardon" (Isaiah 55:7).

But how can a person control his or her thoughts? That is the question. How can an unrighteous person forsake his or her unrighteous thoughts?

Without doubt, God's supernatural power can provide victory for us in Christ. But we must cooperate with that power. A fat man who continues to gorge himself on chocolate cakes and fudge bars while he prays for victory over appetite will not find his prayers answered. Neither will a lustful man who refuses to quit ogling dirty magazines and x-rated videos while he asks God to cleanse his mind.

By beholding we become changed. One key, then, to controlling covetousness and other sinful thoughts is to fill our minds with those things that do not incite such desires. "Finally, brethren, whatsoever things are true, whatsoever things are honest, whatsoever things are just, whatsoever things are pure, whatsoever things are lovely, whatsoever things are of good report; if there be any virtue, and if there be any praise, think on these things" (Philippians 4:8). God will give us victory over covetousness, anger, lust, pride—all the silent inner sins of the soul that only we (and God) know about. But we must cooperate.

No question, you are guilty of Thoughtcrime. Had you lived in Orwell's *1984,* your destiny would be certain. "People simply disappeared, always during the night. Your name was removed from the registrars, every record of everything you had done was wiped out, your one-time existence was denied and then forgotten. You were abolished, annihilated."

Fortunately, Orwell's nightmare fantasy was only that—a fantasy. In reality, we have a loving Creator, an all-powerful God who has no desire to destroy us for our sins. Instead, through Jesus Christ, God offers cleansing and victory and eternal life—to everyone, everywhere, for every sin.

Even for Thoughtcrime.